CALLED

THE CRISIS AND PROMISE
OF FOLLOWING JESUS TODAY

MARK LABBERTON

IVP Books

An imprint of InterVarsity Press
Downers Grove, Illinois

To Steve Hayner,
whose joy infectiously loved me into God's call

InterVarsity Press
P.O. Box 1400, Downers Grove, IL 60515-1426
World Wide Web: www.ivpress.com
Email: email@ivpress.com

©2014 by Mark Labberton

InterVarsity Press® is the book-publishing division of InterVarsity Christian Fellowship/USA®, a movement of students and faculty active on campus at hundreds of universities, colleges and schools of nursing in the United States of America, and a member movement of the International Fellowship of Evangelical Students. For information about local and regional activities, visit intervarsity.org.

Scripture quotations, unless otherwise noted, are from the New Revised Standard Version of the Bible, *copyright 1989 by the Division of Christian Education of the National Council of the Churches of Christ in the USA. Used by permission. All rights reserved.*

While any stories in this book are true, some names and identifying information in this book may have been changed to protect the privacy of individuals.

Cover design: Cindy Kiple
Interior design: Beth Hagenberg
Images: © Pupkis/iStockphoto

ISBN 978-0-8308-3683-3 (print)
ISBN 978-0-8308-9694-3 (digital)

Printed in Canada ∞

Library of Congress Cataloging-in-Publication Data
Labberton, Mark, 1953-
Called : the crisis and promise of following Jesus today / Mark Labberton.
pages cm
Includes bibliographical references.
ISBN 978-0-8308-3683-3 (hardcover : alk. paper)
1. Christian life. I. Title.
BV4501.3.L327 2014
248.4—dc23

2014022810

| P | 21 | 20 | 19 | 18 | 17 | 16 | 15 | 14 | 13 | 12 | 11 | 10 | 9 | 8 | 7 | 6 | 5 | 4 | 3 | 2 | 1 |
| Y | 31 | 30 | 29 | 28 | 27 | 26 | 25 | 24 | 23 | 22 | 21 | 20 | 19 | 18 | 17 | 16 | 15 | 14 |

CONTENTS

A LIFE ABUNDANT

When I was considering the possibility of embracing Christian faith as a young college student, what I feared most was that it would make my life smaller rather than larger—less love, less joy, less creativity, less wonder, less engagement. I had met enough Christians who were incarnational proof of this, so when I finally came to faith in Christ as a college student, it was because I discovered that Jesus saves people *from* the very smallness I feared. I saw that the very essence of the kingdom of God is a life bigger than I would ever find outside of it.

I understand how we have come to live in times where many reject the gospel for being too small, too parochial for the enormous challenges we face. I know very well how it is that the lives of Christians seem too constricted to have any relevance to the real world and its messy complexities, and how far removed the Christian life can appear from abundance, freedom and joy. As a study assistant to the Anglican pastor and writer John Stott during my early years as a believer, I witnessed John's faithfulness in public and private, as a highly visible speaker and as a nearly invisible spiritual shepherd to many. What I saw served to cement my conviction about life abundant as a follower of Jesus.

It was on a trip to India and Bangladesh where, in a dark, dilapidated courtyard surrounded by small fire pits, blackened pots and a group of simple homes housing a handful of people, I heard the global Christian leader give one of his most memorable sermons. I saw that the abundant life I hoped for—that he and those to whom he spoke shared—was carried with them on the inside. Inside, they were not bound; they were no longer small.

John had been asked by a friend, a priest serving in Burma, for a tender and intimate favor: John, he said, I am serving so far away from my dying mother in Madras; you might be able to reach her sooner than I can. She is poor, in declining health, and her teeth are falling out one by one. Would you make a pastoral visit to her the next time you are in India?

And so we set off, with scant information about location, to find his friend's elderly mother. After hours of searching, moving self-consciously through streets of shacks and shelters so different than the more established structures we'd left only three hours before, we arrived at the door to this woman's home. Eventually, she emerged from the shadows, frail but beaming with tearful joy. At her insistence, she knelt at John's feet and kissed them, and then the two of them spoke through our translator for awhile. At the end of our visit, she asked John to speak and to give her a blessing.

A small piece of carpet was honorifically placed for him in the center of the mud floor, and without anything like the kind of pulpit to which he was often accustomed, John preached on John 3:16. It was John Stott at his fullest. Filled with love for Jesus and for his fellow pastor, John spoke to the mother who had believed, in spite of her poverty, not as a stranger but as God's own. The mother who provided such a rich inheritance to her son received the blessing of her son's gratitude as John interceded. His words were simple and clear. His tone was compassionate and dignified. His intellectual rigor and verbal skill were fully intact. And his assurances were personal and tender. He was fully present to her and to the goodness of God. It was the sermon of his life, and it has shaped my view of following Jesus ever since.

That scene was a rich moment of God's grace. A priest in

Burma, a widow in India, a world-renowned British preacher and his young American intern—we were so deeply connected in the family of Christ, by Christ and in Christ that a transcendence beyond all of us and our meager circumstances took place, filling us.

That experience explained the abundant life to me in terms that were heart and mind shaping. It is a life I have come to recognize consistently in many other men and women I have known who follow the common call to live daily as followers of Jesus, whatever their walk of life or part of the world. This is the good news: that God so loved the world that the gift of God's Son reorders and enlarges our hearts and our lives.

Later, John's life was one of the counterpoints that further helped me to see the cosmic and global reach of the gospel. Thousands heard John proclaim on a vast stage, "Our God is a global God." But I heard it in his tiny London flat, in his words, his prayers and his letters. Although God clearly provides gifts for ministry, greater influence comes through character, the fruit of God's Spirit. Charisma, winsomeness, popularity, charm, cleverness can matter. The greater testimony, however, comes from a character shaped by the love of Jesus, consistently demonstrated in ordinary action. I witnessed it equally that day in John's preaching and in the faith of the stooped widow.

The kingdom of God is always intimate but never small. This is what drew and draws people to Jesus. It all turns, however, on our response to Jesus' two words: "Follow me." This is the primary call of God that creates and defines the church. We bear authentic witness to God's love when we demonstrate Jesus-following lives. But too often, we don't. The gift we are meant to be is neither available nor received. Meanwhile the world needs a church that actually lives its call. Urgently.

We will not resolve the crisis from inside the church by devising improved techniques to address denominational disharmony, declining brand loyalty, physical and financial decay, and other alarming trends. That would be like offering swimming lessons in an empty swimming pool. We will not resolve the crisis by personal renewal alone, by asking, "What is God's call on my life?" The question is earnest but individualistic, often neglecting the shared vocation for the people of God.

We can, however, recenter our lives on Jesus Christ, whose call is to "live differently." Whatever our context, our work, our relationships—that is the primary thing we are to be about every day: following Jesus. Our lives unfold daily amid beauty and horror and everything in between. Our opportunities vary widely, as do our commitments. The range of human experience, so outside our control, means that some live in privilege while the far larger measure are subjected to poverty, violence and injustice.

Exquisite life. Suffering life. All of life can be infused with the presence of God; all life matters to the God revealed in the Bible, the Word made flesh in Jesus Christ. God has come among us in Jesus Christ to love and heal us.

The community of God's people—the church—is meant to be an agent of and evidence of that transcendence. This is the crisis and the promise of following Jesus today.

CALLED TO FLOURISH

While on a long flight, I finished listening to my favorite pieces by John Coltrane, then opened some music I had recently downloaded but not yet heard. It was a recording of Vivaldi's *Four Seasons* played by Joshua Bell and the Academy of St. Martin in the Fields. The piece, intense and passionate, has been very important to me over the years. I hadn't noticed that this recording included a short video excerpt of Bell and the orchestra during a recording session, playing an especially dramatic passage. When I opened the file, the video suddenly began to play.

Surprised, I was at once so fully captured and moved by what I saw and heard that it was like I fell into a trance. When it finished, I was breathless. I immediately wanted to ask the flight attendant whether I could use the microphone so I could tell everyone that my life had just been changed. In those three short minutes, I watched and heard what human flourishing means.

On the video, all the musicians, dressed in street clothes that reflected their individual backgrounds and personalities, added their particular instrument and part to the symphonic whole. Each was essential. Each was doing in that moment something very few others could do but that he or she did exceptionally well. Bell, one of the finest violinists in the world, conducted the whole, while also brilliantly playing his exquisite part of Vivaldi's piece. The flourishing was in both the parts and the whole, the individuals and the community.

I have just watched this short piece again, as I've done so many times since that moment on the plane. Each viewing stuns me with wonder at the human imagination that created the piece; the artistic skill, gifts, emotions and discipline that made playing it possible; the community in diversity that made room for each person to be so significant and needed; and the brilliance and leadership of Bell as he both conducted and played.

This is an expression of human flourishing, which is always about the one and the many, about the realization and expression of what is life giving and creative, of what is unique and what is common, of what is passionate and meaningful.

These features of human flourishing are found across cultures and time. They're formal and informal, public and private, common and exceptional. This flourishing happens at home, within families, on the athletic field, in business meetings, in classrooms, in communities of care, in the midst of joy but also of pain, in the context of poverty but also of wealth, in whatever the language or medium or context in which it occurs.

The God made known in Scripture and incarnate in Jesus Christ desires flourishing people in a flourishing world. This is God's intent and commitment, and God created humans to flourish by colaboring with him in that endeavor. Sadly, the narrative of the Bible includes how God's divine desire is subverted by the very human beings God created as partners to reflect God's image and steward creation. Even more, however, it tells the long story of how God relentlessly pursues us in faithfulness and love. God shares with us, out of the flourishing communion of Father, Son and Spirit, the overflow that is our hope and salvation.

You and I are to be the tangible evidence of God's intent for and pursuit of the world today. You and I. Together. The church. This is our calling as followers of Jesus. We are to fulfill the calling of all humanity and thus point to the true purpose of human life. The Word made flesh in Jesus Christ should show through us. We are meant to be primary evidence of the flourishing love, grace and truth in Jesus Christ through the Holy Spirit.

This is why Jesus says his disciples are to be the salt of the earth and the light of the world. The unique and authoritative witness of the New Testament centers on Jesus Christ's life, death and resurrection, and then in the gift of the Holy Spirit. As the Son returns to the Father, he hands the unfolding ministry of the kingdom of God to the people of God (Matthew 28; John 21).

Though the kingdom is God's work by the Spirit, we are not spiritual mannequins—a form without life. We are meant to be active, willful, fruit-bearing agents of that kingdom. The Spirit enables us to live both as ourselves (in honesty and humility) and beyond ourselves (in love and sacrifice). All of this is far from plain in our world. This is why revelation is needed and why our living enactment of that revelation is part of God's purpose.

A Biblical Call

Call is a word that has many associations, so let's be clear what it means here.

The heart of God's call is this: that we receive and live the love of God for us and for the world. This is the meaning of the two great commandments, that we are made to love the

Lord our God with all we are and our neighbors as ourselves. The Bible as a whole, and Jesus in particular, reveals what such a life looks like. Our call is loving communion with God and God's world. It encompasses our identity, our community and our activity.

Who are we? We are God's chosen people, members of a community set apart for God's purposes:

> Now the LORD said to Abram, "Go from your country and your kindred and your father's house to the land that I will show you. I will make of you a great nation, and I will bless you, and make your name great, so that you will be a blessing. I will bless those who bless you, and the one who curses you I will curse; and in you all the families of the earth shall be blessed." (Genesis 12:1-3)

We are people who live in the abundance of God's love and grace, poured out in Jesus Christ:

> I pray that, according to the riches of his glory, he may grant that you may be strengthened in your inner being with power through his Spirit, and that Christ may dwell in your hearts through faith, as you are being rooted and grounded in love. I pray that you may have the power to comprehend, with all the saints, what is the breadth and length and height and depth, and to know the love of

Christ that surpasses knowledge, so that you may be filled with all the fullness of God. (Ephesians 3:16-19)

Why are we here? We are here to love God and to love our neighbor:

"Teacher, which commandment in the law is the greatest?" He said to him, "'You shall love the Lord your God with all your heart, and with all your soul, and with all your mind.' This is the greatest and first commandment. And a second is like it: 'You shall love your neighbor as yourself.' On these two commandments hang all the law and the prophets." (Matthew 22:36-40)

We are here to live in the world as agents of God's love in Jesus Christ:

You are the salt of the earth; but if salt has lost its taste, how can its saltiness be restored? It is no longer good for anything, but is thrown out and trampled under foot.

You are the light of the world. A city built on a hill cannot be hid. No one after lighting a lamp puts it under the bushel basket, but on the lampstand, and it gives light to all in the house. In the same way, let your light shine before others, so that they may see your good works and give glory to your Father in heaven. (Matthew 5:13-16)

God's call encompasses the foundational purposes of our lives and also guidance for life's concrete work and activity. Calling isn't just a category for those who pursue some form of recognized ministry; it's about God's desire for all of our lives as ambassadors of God's kingdom. This is our primary call. This primary call for *all* of us leads naturally and secondarily to God's call for *each* of us.

Not Primarily a Burning Bush

Only once does God's call come from a burning bush. Only once does God speak, even to Isaiah, "on a throne, high and lofty" (Isaiah 6:1). God's primary call is for us to belong to and live for the flourishing of God's purposes in the world. At the same time, God may also call in ways that include direction in relation to such things as jobs, gifts, relationships and more. So, God's call encompasses the foundational purposes of our lives and sometimes provides guidance for our concrete work and activity.

As a result, people ask many questions about how their lives relate to the world. What are our lives in this world about? What are we to make of being human? Why are we here? Is there a reason we are alive, and, if so, how do we know what that is? These questions can be brought on by beauty and joy but also by the daunting facts of our own lives or of the world around us. We look around in doubt, in pain, in suffering. These are human questions asked throughout history by those inside and outside the church.

Today, in a staggeringly complex and diverse world, the overarching biblical narrative that includes creation, fall, redemption and fulfillment has frequently been rejected and denied. The issues seem too many and the evidence too little for them. The secular, street-level view seems the most reliable: humanity is here on its own.

Are we alone in the universe? No god, just us? Do we simply face an empty universe, live a mere biochemical existence, experience what we call pain or joy, and then die? Do we see a world with exquisite natural beauty and think of it as mere materiality with no greater meaning? Do we look upon billions of people who suffer daily at the hands of bullies and tyrants and weigh it only in terms of social consequence or utility? Do we find in apparent acts of self-sacrificing love only the evidence of instinctive, evolutionary social welfare?

And we also ask, "Is there hope?" Is there any reason to think that the trajectory of human suffering and injustice or social entropy can actually be stopped or reversed? Is there hope that the world of poverty, violence and injustice will change? Is there hope that our own personal life issues might actually give way to new life, that our downward spiral can be reversed?

These questions may sound philosophical, but they're personal and practical. In real words and real deeds, God's people are sent as God's reassuring response to these questions. But that can be evident only if we live honestly and fully before God and our neighbor.

WHY CALL MATTERS

If the narrative character of Scripture conveys anything to us, it underlines that God is not a deity of ideas and forms so much as the God of love and relationship. The weight of God's faithful pursuit of creation, of Israel and of the world is conveyed through the story of God speaking, promising, pursuing, calling, engaging, revealing, sustaining, comforting and redeeming. These are tales of grace demonstrated and truth performed. And the verbs above should be our guiding cue regarding call.

The first and second commandments taught by Jesus—to love God and love our neighbor—are our calling. They guide the enactment of life as God intends it to be lived. We find our lives by losing them in these particular ways. We lose our lives, and gain them too, in the *action* of laying them down in worship and love.

The people of God, by the power of the Holy Spirit, are meant to be the hope of the world, the model for all humanity and the apologetic—the living defense of the faith—that God is present and that God's loving purposes will come to pass.

This is the vision and the intent as Jesus portrays it.

Here is the crisis: we've been made and redeemed for this calling, but it slides through our fingers. Jesus' followers live with all the tensions and ambiguities that others do. We see as clearly as others do that often love is as much or even more evident in the lives of unchurched friends or colleagues as it is in those in the church. We say we are following Jesus, but what we actually offer is buildings, programs, music, classes, token work projects and budget appeals.

Our calling has become encrusted, buried under layers that lack significant evidence of life. Viral cat videos seem to touch our humanity and longing more than many church services do. I have felt caught in this vortex. The temptation in the church is to bring in more clowns and light the sparklers, but the real solution is what the Bible declares is our calling: to live out genuine love that shows up in the face of real need.

Making a Difference

At one point, I was involved in a long process of getting clarity from the IRS about a particularly technical and complicated aspect of my taxes. After several months of correspondence and legal advice, the day finally came to begin the talks in person. Those who knew the IRS suggested this would take many months, probably longer, to get settled.

I went to the IRS office in Oakland. I waited. And I waited. Eventually I was escorted through a warren of cubicles to the one where I was to meet the agent who would assist me. Alone in the bowels of a large IRS office—without hope. Yes, I think that captures it.

The agent there listened to my case, took all the relevant paperwork and excused herself to consult with someone else.

I waited ten minutes. Then fifteen minutes. Twenty minutes. Thirty . . . forty . . . forty-five minutes. No one checked in. As far as I could tell, the agent had disappeared. No apparent sign of life—just a cubicle in the void.

Suddenly, the agent was back. She handed me a sheet and said simply, "There, it's all done. It's settled."

I honestly did not know what she meant. I assumed she was saying that she had taken the first step. What she meant was that the whole process was settled. She turned the paper over and revealed the nine signatures she had acquired all the way up the IRS ladder so the case was now closed, and closed in my favor.

There, in the midst of a warren of bureaucratic anonymity and powerlessness, I encountered a person who became my advocate, who heard my appeal and who took the initiative to do on my behalf what I could never have done for myself. She met me at a moment of isolation and fear and sent me out with resolution when I had anticipated nothing but delay.

For me, this has been a parable of what the body of Christ can be in the world. We are to be those who, in the vastness of the universe and in a context of human powerlessness, show up as advocates who represent and incarnate the presence of God, who is the hope of the world.

We can, of course, choose instead to be bureaucrats. Show up and shuffle paper, stand in the shadows, engage very little, have low expectations, put in our time, make sure we get paid all we deserve, watch out for our own interests, demonstrate form without life. In some systems, even this is more than we might be able to do. At the Oakland IRS office, there was a system, but there was a person in the system who was ready to be an advocate. I don't know why, but she did it. And it changed everything for me.

Not every day in our work involves being able to make such a practical difference or to reach such resolution. Likewise, we aren't all meant to be a Joshua Bell and play at St. Martin in the Fields. But we are meant to have a vital role in the company of God's people, who find life by living our call to love and follow Jesus Christ and to love our neighbors as ourselves. As stunningly powerful as Bell's playing is to hear, so life giving is the love we discover as we follow Jesus.

This is the glorious promise of our calling—for us and for the world: to live life abundantly. In Jesus' terms, that means being a people who live in deep, loving communion with the God of the universe, where life has been given away in love so a broken world can flourish.

But instead the church does the polka in a hip-hop world. Perhaps quaint, but clearly disconnected. Teenagers and young adults wander off in disregard, taking their real issues of life, relationships, work and sexuality, and finding some other place and some other community to call home. Others who suffer, such as those confused in their work, anxious for their children or finding the world a weighty burden, wander around for help but have little sense the church is a place to turn. People of all ages who are weary of rhetoric, skeptical of formulas and skeptical of certainty, long for true communion and hope—ingredients for a flourishing life.

The gospel and the church are not the same. But, for many, they are indistinguishable. When God's people fail to live our call, the church buries the gospel. That's where we are. That's the crisis we must face.

PRACTICE

Hearing and living God's call typically develops over time in community. With that in mind, each chapter will include some ways to cultivate that kind of life and practice. These are offered without any intention of implying that a call is automatic, uniform or forced. The process is more likely nuanced and unexpected. But as with spiritual disciplines, God honors our intentionality, and hopefully these practices are invitations into deliberately seeking, reflecting, discerning and practicing God's call—individually and with others.

Where do you experience human flourishing? Music? Art? People? Athletics? Education? Choose a creative medium to help you reflect on flourishing.

- Make a "flourishing collage" using photos, art, words or another medium. Find photos that remind you of contexts other than your own in need of flourishing.

- Assemble a "flourishing playlist." Which songs help you experience flourishing and which remind you of the long road of answering that call? What global or countercultural music could remind you of other areas of the world longing for flourishing?

- Write a list of the areas in your life that are flourishing and another of the areas that are not.

For additional individual and corporate practices, please visit fuller.edu/called to find a six-session study guide, videos and church-based resources. Or to have a conversation with others who are grappling with the issues raised in *Called*, use the hashtag #CALLEDtofollow or follow Mark on Twitter at MLabberton.

A LOST CHURCH
IN A LOST WORLD

His tattoos were flames that licked their way up his neck to his cheekbones. I had caught sight of him only from a distance while I was preaching, a visitor I'd not yet had a chance to meet. But this morning we'd run into each other on the sidewalk, and I'd had a chance to see his artwork up close.

He explained that he was in his late twenties, a grad student at the University of California–Berkeley after a number of years traveling in various bands. He'd recently been asking questions about life that he hadn't considered for a long time, and that had led him back to church.

He said, "I go to some churches, and they talk a lot about Jesus but little about the world. I go to other churches, and they talk a lot about the world but little about Jesus. You seem to talk a lot about Jesus and a lot about the world. I know lots of people like me in this town. I don't need to find more of us. Here's what I want to know: if I hang out at your church, will I meet people who are actually *like* Jesus?"

Put to the Test

Did you wince at that question? Depending on your own church experience, you may have your own response to this provocative inquiry: "Will I meet people who are like Jesus?"

- "Hmm . . . you'll definitely meet people who know they *need* Jesus."

- "You might be interested in visiting the food pantry we run downtown."

- "Before I answer that, tell me a bit more about your religious experience growing up."

It doesn't take research to know that many people, especially in the millennial generation, feel that the Christian church bears little resemblance to the One it claims to follow. Most of us have heard firsthand from those who think Christians act more like judgmental religious fanatics than like Jesus.

It is painful to contemplate that the people of God seem far from flourishing. If we aren't struggling with corruption from within, we're swimming upstream against a culture with increasingly negative views of religious faith. Instead of trying to understand why those views have taken hold, we dismiss them as misunderstandings by people for whom the things of God are foolishness. Or worse, we fight them by staging protests against those we perceive as enemies infringing on our religious rights.

Perhaps the deepest truth is that the church has lost its way in the world. What's more, it doesn't know it.

This is a double crisis for a community that Jesus said is to be the light of the world, the salt of the earth (Matthew 5:13-16). It is a crisis brought on by the failure to be and to do what is most central to the church's identity and purpose: follow Jesus.

Instead of demonstrating the life of Jesus, very different things are seen in the church. According to a Barna Group survey, *homophobic*, *judgmental* and *hypocritical* were three top words used by those outside the church to describe it.[1] Other descriptors don't get much better.

We all have our stories and examples. So many people's rejection or dismissal of the Christian faith turns on anecdotes and experiences of disappointment or offense by the church: Clergy abuse, political manipulation, coercive guilt. The well-known Christian giver who is a jerk or worse in her business practices. The person who always shows up when the doors of the church are open but who lies or gossips much of the time. The person who advocates Christ to others but who advocates mostly for himself.

All of this leads to the following labels for the church, which may be unspoken but that name what many observe and experience.

The self-absorbed church. The church can seem simply self-absorbed. The ordinary congregation often gives the impression it is a small, inwardly fixated club, either bland or full of rivalry and fury inside, with disregard beyond itself. The church can seem as self-enclosed as any other social group, bent in on its own people, purposes and ends, and it rarely has a life of loving engagement and service. What it does beyond itself is "mission," too often an add-on that feels like a project, not the embodiment of humble, loving care. For those called to follow the One whose life was self-giving love, the church can seem self-absorbed, working some angle for its own benefit. Its vocation seems to be with itself.

The invisible church. In contrast, but no better, the average church can also seem functionally invisible—culturally or emotionally or socially. The ordinary presence and activity of the church seems to leave little relevant imprint—even of presence, let alone of compassion. It's a cipher. People drive by the tens of thousands to church buildings, plain or adorned, unkempt or tidy, and may be aware of some general sense of church as a landmark or a weekly parking nuisance, but the increasing secularism of North American culture means the church seems as dated as most Elks Clubs or Order of Odd Fellows. Its vocation seems irrelevant.

The oppressive church. If awareness of the church exists, news headlines leave the impression that the church is an oppressive influence on life. It's associated with offensive headlines from outspoken, often caustic, self-appointed Christian voices who want to impose their hostile or antiquated views on others. This church is like a specter that occasionally crosses people's paths and that many hope will not stay long. The impression people can get is that Christians have an absorbing interest in things that don't matter much to those outside it and are passionately divided over issues that do concern it. This should tell us we are in a tailspin. To many, the church appears to be a fight club, and a boring one at that. Its vocation seems divisive and offensive.

The siloed church. Though the people of God are meant to be evidence of a new and unexpected humanity—"no longer Jew or Greek, there is no longer slave or free, there is no longer male and female; for all of you are one in Christ Jesus"—the church is one of the most ethnically segregated institutions (Galatians 3:28). The same can be said about class or subculture. Local churches are often microcosms of the same sociology as any other part of life and bear little evidence of the new humanity Jesus seeks. Many outside the church do far better at living across "the dividing walls" of hostility (Ephesians 2:14) than those of us who are meant to show the way.

The bad-news church. In addition, the church claims to hold good news, but it's not apparent that such "news" is real or significant, let alone "good." It seems commonplace to deduce that much of what the church announces as news is stale. In a world of endless news cycles, *new* and *news* are ready synonyms. "The old, old story of Jesus and his love" doesn't grab attention; there's nothing new there—even if it is true. And the truthfulness of it all seems weak or unstable. The truth of the gospel has shifted in the minds of many from something that is about fact, like a heliocentric universe, to something more akin to an aesthetic claim, like the beauty of a sunrise. Again, the news quality slips, and its significance slips with it.

The no-news church. From a wider cultural perspective, "good" is a matter of taste, not of moral reality. On either an individual or a social level, the "good news" reflected in the history of the church seems to be incidental and unnecessary. Amid an array of moral convictions, the indistinguishable character of the church undermines its claims of a superior—indeed ontologically true—moral vision. On the broad public level, the spectacular failures of the church's leaders discredit its claims of "goodness." When the Christian next door demonstrates the same self-interested, consumer life as anyone else, goodness seems like a faint sentimentality.

The good-news church. What would it take to become the good-news church? For the church today to claim it knows the Way, it needs to demonstrate convincingly that it has good news deserving of that name. In a world of violence, of fear, of poverty, of injustice, it has to show up in relationships and actions of life-giving power. In other words, the church has to show a different view and practice of power than the world around us displays. It has to show it knows the Way in a time of explosive global change and confusion.

THE WAY

This critique is not coming from a cheap critic looking in from the outside but from someone who feels privileged to have been a pastor for thirty years. I love what pastoral ministry involves, especially the earthiness of people's real experiences of life and of God, of faith and of doubt, across all seasons of life. I believe the local church can be one of the best contexts in which to be formed as a person and as a disciple.

And I too often find the church to be a place of deep disconnection and disappointment. For all the reasons just named, we are indistinguishable and irrelevant far, far too much of the time. As I drive by church buildings and read Christian magazines and go to Christian websites, I'm struck by what feels like the presence of an ecclesiastical-industrial complex rather than the aroma of Jesus Christ.

Today one of the best things the church could do is listen to its critics and, in light of following Jesus, ask again, "How are we meant to live?"

With grace and hope, the church is to inherently and commonly seek and love the forgotten, the unseen, the undesirable, the uncool. We need to do so with unexpected, tangible love, displaying counterintuitive compassion (including enemy-love) and demonstrating a capacity for magnanimous forgiveness, mercy and justice.

This is Jesus' way.

God intends for the church to be a community of love and hope in a lost world. But when our life is nothing more than the lost among the lost, what happens to the light and the salt?

The Lost World

The dire situation of the church might not matter so much if the world in which it is placed and for which it exists were not lost too. But it is. Of course, the people of God share the same realities. Despite Jesus' warning, God's people are in and of the world. Pain, suffering, disease, confusion, economic turmoil, religious hostilities, violence, failed leadership, personal and institutional fear, and technological tyrannies are rife around the world—and therefore in the experience of God's people too. We are participants, not victims, in this situation.

Just as the church can be tagged with certain labels, so can the culture of which we are a part.

The free-floating life. We live in a world that has an ever-increasing number of people who feel that life bobs on currents of the moment. The sea is open and wide. Questions of direction, purpose or meaning seem indulgent. This leaves many with an exhilarating sense of freedom. Without the tether of encumbering expectations and boundaries of tradition, some find this free-floating life to be the kind of creative and self-created world they believe to be most natural and fruitful. In such circumstances, the imposition of external values or traditions slides away. The individual can assert or create (or not) as she wishes. Not all sailing will be easy, of course, but it holds the possibility of sailing as one wishes and not being hampered by traditional entanglements and obligations. A common social contract evaporates.

The vertigo life. For others, the free-floating life fosters vertigo. Or it feels like a free fall; the sensation is not exhilaration but terror. The lack of order or direction promotes anxiety and paralysis, or at least fear. This can lead to an adamant effort to find or assert fixed points for orienting life. A mirage will do, even if it's only that. It may quiet the fear, but the free fall is just a flash away. When we feel lost, we assume there's a way to find home, but when there's no home, we're left with wandering.

The pinged life. Life through the Internet contains an endless set of unsorted pings. These prompts demand our attention, successfully or not, and present us with a perpetual onslaught of distractions and diversions. Invisible algorithms of advertising or advocacy, or of friends and acquaintances, ping into our lives all sorts of information, opportunities and appetites. Our lives can easily become the story of how we respond to this endless set of prompts.

Our pinged existence is a universe of associations and initiatives that are technologically generated, and we may or may not seek or have any degree of control. When writers suggest that Google makes us stupid, they're talking about the effects of the pinged life. It turns out not to be neutral in its impact. Rather, it fosters a diminished capacity for sustained attention, for careful listening, for discernment of interpersonal communication and for observation and reflection.

The lonely life. At a time of exponential social networking, loneliness is no stranger. Our global population may exceed seven billion, but feeling alone has probably never been more common. Science demonstrates again and again that our physical health and well-being are directly correlated to the quality of our relations with others. We long to know and be known, but our fears and habits make it difficult to give or receive love. We feel vulnerable to injury in relationships, and we often keep our stories of struggle or confusion to ourselves. So we may try various strategies short of actually and freely loving, but the consequence is relationships that don't last or don't satisfy, or both. More and more people choose proximity without intimacy. Our hearts are heavy and alone.

The imposter's life. Appearance more than substance seems to be our contemporary preference. The eye is the critical dimension. What matters most is what we *seem* to be. We doubt that much beyond appearance can be found anyway, so it's easier and more immediate to settle for the imposter's life. This is cued by the willingness to forgo all the details in favor or simply affirming "it's all good" and moving on. This means you can just go on from where you are with no distracting baggage, no entanglements or complications. This is different from actually being a poser—someone who wants to be something they are not. The imposter's life is simply not full of pretense; it allows someone to think about us the way they want without actually disclosing who we really are. Since "it's all good," there's nothing to worry about.

The ironic life. This is the life of the protected idealist: the one who wishes life would be as she longs for it to be but who protects herself from disappointment with "it doesn't matter" or "I knew anyway" or "it's what I thought." This approach guards against naiveté, against being taken in, against vulnerability, against being hurt. No one starts life as an ironist; it's the harvest of disappointment. When the battering of reality just gets to be too much, this is a good place to be, because it thickens the barrier of self-protection while sometimes making you seem very present and alive. That's the one thing the ironic life is not: alive. The lack of real life comes from the layering that keeps experience at a distance. That's not life as much as it is a survival strategy.

The consumer life. Life isn't about who you are but about what you have, because what you have tells you who you are. This is the consumer life. What we pursue as consumers of culture, of goods, of experience, of taste are the things that feed our consumption and increase our desire for still more. Marketers know this. Google, the largest advertising company in the world, builds its business on knowing us so as to sell to us, for to sell to us is to know us. Apple's Steve Jobs said that people don't even know what they want until they're shown: what we consume tells us what we desire.[2]

The fearful life. Real and imagined dangers exist all around us. The forces of nature and society, the influences of individuals and systems, the invisible activities of everything from germs to drugs to terrorists threaten with genuine danger. There's a feeling of inadequate power or control. Some experience this as the baseline for most days. For others, it's an undulating cycle that's always present and occasionally fierce. This fearful life can be paranoid or obsessive. Fear can be tamed but is readily accessed with the right triggers just a flashpoint away: getting it wrong, not being seen, being hurt, experiencing violence, losing control, failing, getting overlooked, doing damage, causing pain, misspeaking.

These are each, and all together, symptoms of many of our lives. We live in circumstances that may be privileged or deprived, but these frightening themes frequently set the agenda for our lives. This is true for those who regard themselves inside or outside the church. Few of these patterns of life are different either way.

DOUBLE LOSTNESS

The lostness of the world—"having no hope and without God in the world"—is a biblical assumption (Ephesians 2:12). We don't assume that the people of God—the light and salt of the world—would seem as lost as others. Yet this is the crisis before us.

When the church fails to remember its identity and to

practice it in ways that land in the context of the real world, the primary means God has chosen to bear witness to God's love, mercy and justice is confused and stifled. Although many Christians and some congregations do live their calling in context, the evidence is that most do not.

We must face up to the enormous loss of credibility between the faith the church professes and the actions we demonstrate. Nothing else should matter to the church of Jesus Christ as much as this.

This is not a book about how to find the job or spouse or activity that will most fully maximize the real you. In fact, that approach is part of what we need to reconsider. And it isn't a step-by-step manual on "knowing the will of God for your life" in the very individualized way many pursue. Rather, we will reflect here on the identity and calling that God has given the church and on what we must not only recover but also practice. It will involve practicing our faith in a context that we need to acknowledge and understand as radically changed.

A Simple and Essential Goal

The people of God must face this crisis: the church is losing its mission in the world. The root of the problem lies not outside the church but inside: we're failing to live our calling in specific ways that we need to acknowledge and understand.

Every believer and every community of believers needs to recover our identity as followers of Jesus and learn to practice it in daily life, in the context of the real world.

In this, we find our life. And so does our world.

PRACTICE

Set aside an hour or so to take a prayer walk through the neighborhood surrounding a place where you spend a good deal of time—your home, church, workplace, school or shopping center, for example.

- As you walk, pray that God would help you see people, activities and life experiences in this neighborhood that you may not have noticed.

  - What people, buildings or other observations stand out to you?

  - What does this walk suggest to you about the questions, doubts or fears your neighbors may carry?

  - Which are the people or situations that you imagine Jesus engaging with?

  - In what ways may you, your own church or the universal church be missing a call to this community?

- Pause to pray for specific individuals, activities or circumstances God places on your heart as you walk.

- Choose one or two of these people or circumstances to pray for regularly in the coming weeks and months.

- Return to this neighborhood as often as you are able and pay attention to the ways in which your observations, prayers and interactions change over time.

3

THE PRIMARY CALL

As if from out of nowhere, Pope Francis arrives. In a moment, in the twinkling of an eye, the man who most represents the institutional church and its global identity is on the scene. In the first days of his papacy, the world watches as he washes feet, cares for the poor and reaffirms the basic vocation of the church as the presence of Christ in the world—and everyone is shocked. Out of the layered intrigue of ecclesial power and defensiveness, of word craft and posturing, suddenly we see what we didn't expect: a genuine disciple of Jesus.

The cynical media that so readily and understandably hovers around, exposes and scoffs at the church was stunned and then charmed. Many of us inside the church—Roman Catholic, Protestant, Orthodox or independent—have been as well. Around the world and across denominations, people are taking note that here is a person who doesn't just represent churchly power but who lives what the church professes to be its call. It was enough of a shock for *TIME* magazine to make Pope Francis its Person of the Year for 2013. Why? He simply lives as a follower of Jesus. And that, it turns out, matters.

As Pope Francis vividly and simply portrays, the most urgent call upon the church is simply to live as followers of Jesus. Christendom no longer masks the church's failure to live this primary call. This is the way *Rolling Stone* magazine captured it:

> [Given his reign and persona,] Francis' basic mastery of skills like smiling in public seemed a small miracle to the average Catholic. But he had far more radical changes in mind. By eschewing the papal palace for a modest two-room apartment, by publicly scolding church leaders for being "obsessed" with divisive social issues . . . by devoting much of his first major written teaching to a scathing critique of unchecked free-market capitalism, the pope revealed his own obsessions to be more in line with the boss' son.[1]

It's true that many important, complex factors need to be considered at a time like this. In a postmodern, post-Christian, multireligious landscape, intellectual questions need to continue to receive vigorous intellectual investigation and reflection. Christian orthodoxy must not bury its head and keep saying its creeds without us asking ourselves what is meant and what is heard when we make such fundamental affirmations of faith.

How the church communicates its message, how it tells and lives "the old, old story," and why and how that story matters today is all part of the work the church needs to do. How churches organize themselves and whether they snap, crackle and pop in the way some think they should is not primarily about money, size or technology. The issues are more basic: will the church embody and articulate its only legitimate identity? Will God's people live as followers of Jesus?

No one calls for the church to be less like Jesus—actually, quite the opposite. So it's ironic that what Pope Francis does draws such dramatic attention. What he does is meant to be the daily, pervasive action of the most ordinary Christian disciples. But it's shocking because it seems so unusual.

This fundamental disconnection should trouble the church more than its theological or metaphysical issues, more than its political or ethical debates, more than its ecclesiastical and institutional crises. It's a vocational crisis: is the church remembering and practicing its calling to follow Jesus?

The passionate and enthusiastic response across the religious and political spectrum to the simple witness of Pope Francis seems to expose something fundamental about the state of the church. Who would have thought that someone representing the church actually lived like its namesake and Lord? That is its own wakeup call for all who claim to be disciples.

Everyone is given the gift of living in light of God's call. The church is meant to be the community that chooses to do so and that speaks and acts in ways that call others to do so too. This is the vocation of God being lived through the vocation of the church for the sake of the vocation of the world.

Sometimes the church is just odd: habits, speech, attitudes, potlucks, whatever. Every church is something particular, and you smell it the moment you're on the premises. The point isn't whether a church is odd, but whether it's odd because it imitates Jesus Christ. Does the church live that vocation? Surely this plain and unadorned question is the one that people inside, and certainly outside, the church want to have answered. If the response is anything but yes, we have to ask ourselves what we're doing and why.

Few outside the church measure it by a standard of perfection. What they seek is far, far more achievable: authentic people whose proclamation of their trust in Jesus is backed up by their ordinary but self-giving acts of grace, justice and compassion.

Our Vocation Is Here and Today

The vocation of every Christian is to live as a follower of Jesus today. In every aspect of life, in small and large acts, with family, neighbors and enemies, we are to seek to live out the grace and truth of Jesus. This is our vocation, our calling. Today.

In relation to this primary calling, all the rest is secondary. It matters, but not as much as this vocation. Gifts, context, challenges, personality—these affect how we embody and enact our following of Jesus. Such things have all kinds of impact on how we live out our imitation of Jesus. But they are not the call itself.

Put simply, Jesus extended the same call to all his disciples: "Follow me." Peter wasn't Matthew, who wasn't James or John. Each followed Jesus in a manner unique to his own life, but they had the same basic vocation. This is the clear, galvanizing call upon those who would be disciples.

If we're going to follow, we always begin where we are. If

we're "mending our nets"—that is, going about our daily business as the disciples were—it's precisely there that our following of Jesus starts. This vocation assumes continuity and context. We aren't disciples in midair without bodies, histories, personalities, relationships and much more. We begin to follow by responding to Jesus' invitation where we are.

But as we begin, or continue, we know that we are going in a direction and engaging in things that alter our purpose and reorder our priorities. This usually means doing so right in the midst of the contexts we already inhabit. The continuity is that we start where we are. The discontinuity is that we live and love differently right where we are.

Each of us is a child of parents, perhaps a sibling to someone, a friend to friends, a colleague to coworkers. Following Jesus starts here. It starts with learning to see these people again for the first time, now visible to us anew as we learn to see them as made and loved by God, see their lives whole and seek their flourishing.

This typically brings us face-to-face with the challenges of our vocation. We don't see people this way when they're annoying to us or clearly self-interested or rejecting us and our faith or failing to do their share of the work. Right there, in the midst of ordinary life, we face the gritty task of following Jesus by learning to love and serve those at our doorstep. This will be true throughout our lives as disciples. We will never be called to do less than this. And sometimes this is the hardest part of all.

We might want to rush on to some other dimension of our vocation as followers. We might want to ask, what is God's call for our lives in a larger sense? What is the big picture? What is the adventure of faith to which we're called? But whatever else that call involves, it always includes God's call for where we are today. It's the particularity and imminence of God's love. Jesus demonstrates this in his response to a specific woman who on a specific day was caught in adultery; he calls specific disciples; specific children come to him; a specific leper cries out for help. These are what the day—any day, even today—presented to Jesus! We are called to follow Jesus in relation to what is presented to us. Today.

In the life of the church, this kind of Jesus-following life and love is often forgotten or demoted. This essential vocation seems to get lost. Instead, the roles associated with power, the attention to structures, the organization of programs, the advocacy efforts and other tasks define the church. All of that is just housekeeping detail if the vocation of simply following Jesus in loving God and neighbor is not primary. This is akin to building a house but never building a home. In Jesus' language, we are meant to be seeking the kingdom of God. Living and practicing who and why we are Jesus followers is our Christian vocation. This means remembering our identity and living it out.

KINGDOM VISION

"The kingdom of heaven has come near," Jesus said (Matthew 4:17). This is because he himself had come near. The reign of God's love, mercy and justice came near in Jesus. Emmanuel. Everything is the same, and everything is different.

The full vocation of the church is to follow Jesus in the declaration and enactment of the kingdom. This involves all we are and all we have. It's a call into nothing less than God's work of re-creation, in which all things will be made new.

As far reaching as this vocation is, it is played out in the small and the ordinary as well as in the large and the exceptional. Our gifts and context help shape our contributions, but even before we know what those are, even before God gives clarity to our focus or concentration in kingdom life, even before we have a namable "job" or "mission," we are called to imitate Jesus Christ. As Blaise Pascal said so well, "Do little things as if they were great, because of the majesty of Jesus Christ who does them in us, and who lives our life; and do the greatest things as though they were little and easy, because of his omnipotence."[2]

Following Jesus this day, in the life we are living right now— this is the vocation we must grasp and exercise.

Practice

Choose a statement of faith (such as the Apostles' Creed or another creed, song or prayer) that is familiar to you and/or your worshiping community.

- Read it through several times, pausing to consider each line.

  - In your journal or notebook, write out the first line or affirmation.

  - Write a paragraph or two about your understanding of what this affirmation means for your day-to-day life.

  - Describe how you see yourself living out, or failing to live out, this affirmation.

  - Describe the ways your worshiping community is actively engaging, or failing to engage, these affirmations.

  - Repeat the process for each line of the statement.

- Write a prayer confessing personal and communal failures in action as well as thanksgiving for positive engagement.

- Invite God's guidance as you work to discern how you might more fully put your faith into action.

4

RELOCATING

Where Are We Called?

To follow Jesus, we need to get straight about some things that can entangle our discipleship. Let's start with where we think we live.

None of us hears Jesus' call in a neutral context. The way we see and engage the world or think about our actions or evaluate our possible response to our Lord is set in motion by things that may be invisible to us—powerful things we take for granted and seldom question.

We hold assumptions that can imperil our ability to respond to Jesus' call. To get clearer about the meaning of our call to live as followers of Jesus, we need to reorient ourselves.

Waking to Where We Live

Hearing God's call happens in a context. It starts with where we live. Every setting has its complications, and that is certainly true for the church in the West. A great theme in the identity of the United States is shaped against the backdrop of the exodus narrative. Many in America believe they live in the Promised Land. We say to ourselves, we don't live *there* like we used to or like some still do. We live *here* in the land of milk and honey, in the land of potential and hope, of fulfillment and satisfaction. Whether inside or outside the church, the American Dream is a common theme in our culture, whether our migration was from Europe, Latin America, Asia, Africa or elsewhere.

This Promised Land narrative is one of the two great paradigms in the Hebrew Scriptures. It defines Israel's identity and home, and it undergirds its common life. The same is true for the life of the church: Jew and Gentile, male and female, slave and free have all been invited from death into life, from bondage into freedom (Galatians 3:28). Promised Land life is to be ours.

This biblical narrative is often related to the immigrant story in the founding of the United States. It also serves the secular idea not of a religious Promised Land but of a context for opportunity.

The whole notion is that those in the United States are people who seek life, liberty and happiness. Life and liberty are the pretext for our entitlement of happiness. If the first two are more or less in place, happiness seems like our just desserts. We live in a setting that is free. We are in a context in which we should get to be or to have what we desire.

For the church in North America, such a national narrative can easily mean we are the church of the American Dream. And often the American Dream shapes our church identity, practice and vocation more than anything else. If we're part of the dominant culture in the United States (typically white, educated, middle or upper middle class), we're groomed to think optimistically about our lives and our future. Our faith is often seen as a means to fulfill this dream.

Meanwhile, American culture bids the church to sustain itself on the goods and products, values and experiences of its marketplace. This ever-changing, ever-available market lures and attracts its share of buyers. Our consuming habits offer us another step toward the Promised Land. This is the land of milk and honey.

Seeking, dressing, feeding, decorating and entertaining—buying!—in the Promised Land capture the imagination of the American church. Christian consumers in the United States are virtually indistinguishable from the culture at large.

The intertwining of Promised Land assumptions and consumer opportunities easily becomes a powerful economic, social and spiritual engine. Promised Land hopes fire American consumerism, and the result is very big business.

Our pursuit of the "right" church is an example of this. Church shopping isn't just a metaphor. It's a way of approaching a life of faith that is mostly driven by our consumer instincts. This puts the "buyer" in the controller's seat with expectations and demands, largely in service of personal ends. "How do I find joy, love, happiness, peace, friends, a spouse, a home, a job, safety, security?" It's as though the fruit of the Spirit is comestibles.

This approach makes pragmatic sense if you believe you live in the Promised Land and assume it exists for your benefit. You simply take what's available, which is what you see everyone else doing.

When the Promised Land becomes the Land of Plunder, when blessings are the end and their purpose is forgotten or rejected, all that's left is a shell unable to sustain the life it was meant to foster. The blessings become like sterile fruit. No seed. No greater or deeper end. The Promised Land is gutted.

If this were the evidence of secular culture, a rejection or forgetfulness of God by those who do not believe or trust God, it might describe the counterpoint to a Christian vision of the world. But if instead it's a void that Christians have taken into their own vision of promise and blessings, it creates a crisis.

The premise of God's Promised Land to Israel was not that it was a place to pluck God's benefits. It was rather where God's people were to thrive in the grace of living out the call to be God's people. For Israel, blessings were not the goal; they were the encouragement along the path of living God's way.

However, the major and minor prophets came to announce to the people of Israel that their lives had become inverted, bent in on themselves in ways that meant they sought their own ends rather than God's.

> Yet day after day they seek me
>   and delight to know my ways,
> as if they were a nation that practiced righteousness
>   and did not forsake the ordinance of their God;
> they ask of me righteous judgments,
>   they delight to draw near to God.
> "Why do we fast, but you do not see?
>   Why humble ourselves, but you do not notice?"
> Look, you serve your own interest on your fast day,
>   and oppress all your workers. (Isaiah 58:2-3)

The cost of losing their vocation is the loss of their Promised Land, which is swallowed and consumed by Babylon. Now, instead of living in a context marked by the signs of promise and faithfulness, they live in exile, and everything is changed. It might look familiar, but the basic assumptions are different.

I believe the people of God live in exile. The tantalizing possibilities of getting lost in Promised Land visions live on for many, of course, but others are increasingly realizing it is a mirage. Meanwhile, exile—life as strangers in a strange land—is our context. We have allowed and contributed to a dominant secular culture that has now engulfed us and in which we are ever more fully the minority. We are a declining cultural force against countervailing pressures of spiritual decline. The church of Christendom is fading and flailing.

Living our call in exile involves adjusting to very different circumstances and reading the signals of our environment and culture very differently. It means choosing to give ourselves to those around us with fewer and different expectations, not as settlers but as guests or visitors. We don't whine about the world being the world. We are instead called to love it out of the integrity of our lives, without making our love dependent on its changing. "Seek the welfare [or shalom] of the city, . . . for in its welfare you will find your welfare," is the instruction of Jeremiah 29:7. "If you love those who love you, what reward do you have? Do not even the tax collectors do the same?" Jesus said. "But I say to you, Love your enemies and pray for those who persecute you" (Matthew 5:46, 44).

The church can't live its vocation if it doesn't know where it lives. The culture tells us we are free agents and must construct any meaning our lives may have. It tells us we are what we eat, what we wear, what we weigh, what we own, what we do or what we know.

To our surrounding culture, the voices of the church that complain about secularism can sound like a child having a tantrum. It's like complaining that today is not yesterday or that pain is difficult. Our call is not lived out in the midst of idealism but in the midst of the real world as it is. We're complicit in our society's problems, while at the same time we're called to live redemptively as Jesus' followers. To do so wisely and faithfully, we must face where we live.

THE GIFT OF EXILE

The gift of exilic living, for Israel and now for the North American church, is that it exposes believers to the shoals of authentic faith. When raw reality shoves its way out and demands response, we're given a gift that can change our faith. In the Promised Land vision, we long to get rid of the dissonance and get the majority of people and circumstances to fit our tastes and values. If we instead admit and understand that we live in exile, we realize that the challenges to authentic faith and unexpected love are real and costly. They don't go away in a flash. They are here to stay. They tell us we aren't home. This is the bad news that a good-news people must hear and engage. Otherwise, the good news is not worthy of the name.

When we as Christian believers ask about our calling in light of exile, our expectations suddenly change. We realize that the starting point for our lives isn't in the hothouse of protected faith but in a place of winds and rains and flood that "blew and beat against that house" (Matthew 7:27). This context is already the norm in many parts of the world where being part of a minority population is assumed (Asia, Europe, North Africa, the Middle East and so on—that is, a very large percentage of the world). A vital spiritual life in such circumstances develops out of different practices exercised under very different conditions.

This is surely what Jesus had in mind as he instructed his disciples under the tyrannous rule of Rome. The images of being light in a dark world or salt in a decaying one assume the depth of the need to be great and the difference between God's people and the surrounding world to be dramatically evident. The images Jesus used suggest a qualitative distinction and the provision of something that isn't otherwise available. What we are to add can make a world of difference, but that will be so only if we don't hide our light or lose our saltiness. And these are not just theoretical dangers, it turns out.

LIVING BEYOND OURSELVES

Cultivating a spirituality for exile means learning to live inside-out. It isn't a mere interior spirituality, and the end-point isn't just spiritual survival. Living as faithful strangers in a strange land means providing an essential good for the benefit of the surrounding people or context. The Christian cultural cries go up: "Oh, the movies today! Oh, the politicians today! Oh, the media today!" To blame the world for its own lack of salt or light is ludicrous. "First take the log out of your own eye," cautions Jesus (Matthew 7:5).

This was the point of exile for Israel: they were to seek the shalom of the city in which they were oppressed, for in its shalom they would find their shalom (Jeremiah 29:7). This is the irony that bears the marks of the God of Israel, which is later revealed in Jesus Christ and is now meant to be embodied in the life of the church. The irony is that God's love is not dependent on things going well; rather, it is love given "while we still were sinners" (Romans 5:8). In the Sermon on the Mount, Jesus suggests it's no great accomplishment to believe and follow Jesus when things are going well (see Matthew 6:25-34). Rather, what do you believe and do when the signs of God's faithfulness are less visible?

This is the great heart of God's saving love, which was given by God when the economics of love were all stacked against humanity, when our lovability was the least apparent, when the chances of rescue from our circumstances seemed least probable or least deserved. Paul says, "But God, who is rich in mercy" gave us all we needed (Ephesians 2:4). This is the irony of undeserved love. First, God's love saves us from ourselves, and second, God's love sends us to offer that very love to our fellow undeserving neighbors and friends—from the undeserving to the undeserving.

Living in exile means living beyond ourselves. Because this lifestyle is the inversion of our consumer-oriented culture, we need to dig up the old signposts and replace them with new markers for making wise choices. Let's start with one of the most entrenched myths: life is about succeeding.

Not About Winning

God's strategy is to use unexpected people to embody unexpected love. This means life is not about winning. That's a problem, both for those inside and those outside the church. So much social power is about getting what we want, and what we want is often measured over and against what others get and want. This is social adrenaline. By contrast, the internal irony of God's countercompetitive approach grates against the presuppositions of our winning-obsessed culture. It expects the greatest works from those whose call comes in weakness, not strength. "The greatest among you will be your servant" (Matthew 23:11). This means shifting both the expectations of outcome and the nature of power, and no group of people does either very well.

Power, while seldom morally neutral, can be a necessary good. Using power toward individuals and social good is not only a legitimate way to live but also can and should be part of a specifically Christian way of living.

When the apostle Paul says, "Let the same mind be in you that was in Christ Jesus" (Philippians 2:5), we begin to see how much the Jesus Way leads us into an exilic faith that isn't about winning against the opposition but about loving the opposition in the face of real cost. That's a very different spiritual vision than presupposing that God wants, maybe even guarantees, our success. That approach, however common in some preaching and some church building, is hard to find in the Bible.

Not About Having It All

Promised Land spirituality expects it all and expects it now. Exilic spirituality has to make peace with the partial rather than the whole. In contrast to the Promised Land—which has a kind of comprehensive beneficence, a sense that all things could somehow be right (even if not yet fully so)—exilic life is shaped out of remnants. The temple is gone, but prayer is still available. The vessels are desecrated, but our bodies are a vessel for God. The national rituals are no more, but rhythms of mind, body and spirit can lead us to see and feel and know now "in part."

A friend of mine was a frugal widow with an extraordinarily expansive mind. She had little means but a great love of classical paintings. As a bit of a wayfarer, she decided early on that, as a matter of cost and portability, she would collect stamps that were reproductions of major pieces of classical art. I learned this when she invited me to come and see her "art gallery." Having not been to her home before, I had no idea what to expect, but after I sat down in her living room, she said, "I'm eager to show you some of the great art of the world. Here is my gallery." She pointed to the thick volume on the coffee table. And so it was.

The whole in the part was her way of life. She taught me this in many forms and gave me an example of a person who held her bearings in the midst of a lost marriage, an unfinished career and much uncertainty. She was a person in exile. In the midst of what could have been barren land, she showed me a rich world of profound joy and love.

NEW CUES FOR COMMUNITY

To live the way my friend did requires finding God's presence and assurance in places that we don't anticipate. It means taking the cues of our vocation from signs that aren't fully developed.

This helps significantly when looking for Christian community. Dietrich Bonhoeffer said that one of the first things we need to do is let our expectations of one another in the body of Christ and of the church die. Only then can we begin to find God as the source of our common life—a communion that only God can create or sustain. Promised Land churches offer you everything. An exilic community offers much less and invites you to bring all you can to the community itself.

For those who have grown up in Promised Land churches, this can be difficult to accept. It can seem that we have lost too much or that we can't find the place where things are familiar and fit in place. That's because Christian communities can't be managed so tightly, planned so well or standardized so readily. Instead, we find ourselves among other exiles, people in transition, people not sure where or what fitting in might look like—or even whether that would be a good thing.

Another place where we have to look for different cues is corporate worship. An exilic worshiping community asks more of us than we may be used to giving. The people with us may be less like us: they may have more needs, and they may be less acculturated to the churchy-pleasantness we might be accustomed to. All this holds the possibility of a more authentic community, but it can take practice to find God in the midst of our difference and not just bemoan the more wearing parts of the adjustment. We may say we want to be part of a vigorously multiethnic congregation and that we want it to be economically mixed, but this can make church more complicated. It means adjusting our expectations.

These kinds of differences may mean that simplicity or beauty or consistency wanes. It may mean we find ourselves not feeling as at home as we have in another setting. Right in those moments, we have to ask ourselves what we're looking for and what it will take to make peace with the cues of exile rather than Promised Land. Being and feeling and living as "other" is part of our identification with the love and mercy of Jesus Christ, even if our congregational sociology has mostly done the opposite for much of its life.

Learning how to love and serve in a community of Christian exiles is the pretext for developing and maturing as those who can better love and serve in the wider world of people beyond the life of the church. We can make progress in honesty and mutual submission, patience and empathy—essential ingredients to loving well, especially when loving a stranger.

I watched this happen in particularly moving ways when people living on the street or with mental illnesses or with really poor social skills came into the community of First Presbyterian Church of Berkeley. They were invited into the life we shared, into small groups, into social outings, into service in the community. These relationships weren't usually natural for the super-high-achieving grad student or mid-career professional, but they were authentic and caring examples to me of living as real disciples.

If our experience of these capacities to love develops in Christian community, it means we will have far better instincts and abilities to read and respond to the needs for love in our neighborhoods and workplaces. These are not natural capacities, since our family backgrounds shape our abilities and inabilities to empathize and to love. We need the help of other followers of Jesus to teach us how to love and how to serve beyond our basic skills.

Mary Gordon, the founder of the Roots of Empathy Project, took the need to teach empathy to children so seriously that she developed a program that became a national curriculum in Canada and has now spread to other countries, including the United States. The process of exposing children carefully, deliberately and lovingly to a newborn infant's development in the first months of life has been shown in double-blind tests to make a permanent difference in the lives of those who experience it.

We who follow Jesus Christ are called to be the incarnation of empathy in the name of the One we serve. So where are the double-blind studies that confirm that those who follow Jesus have been changed by the compassion we have been shown? Where is it evident that our empathy shows up beyond the classroom of our discipleship and is apparent in all the real places where love is so desperately needed and desired?

If our vocation has credibility, it has to be road tested, and that means learning and responding to new cues about the work and thought and creativity and mercy we must demonstrate in the midst of exile.

Practice

Over the next several days, keep a journal, notepad or smartphone app nearby to make two lists: one for Promised Land living and another for life in exile.

- Keep track of daily experiences that reflect these two narratives. For example:

  - What activities demonstrate how you hold, exercise or long for power?

- What triggers your desire to win or to be better, stronger, faster?

- What are your consumer habits?

- Which of your expectations are primarily about your own welfare? Which are about the welfare of others?

- Compare your two lists and consider what areas of your life may benefit from looking for "new cues" (see pp. 62-65).

- Prayerfully consider one or two ways you might look for opportunities to seek the shalom of your city through your daily activities, whether at work, home, school or elsewhere.

5

REORIENTING

How Are We Called?

We all know the divide between intentions and actions. What we believe and say may be quite different from what we do. All of us fail to practice what we believe is right.

This tendency is a particular crisis for the people of God, because the church is, after all, God's *ecclesia*—the called-out community that is to be God's arms and legs, voice and touch in the world. The Christian life is to be an incarnational life. The essence of the Christian gospel is the demonstration, the enactment of God's redeeming love. The evidence of the good news landing in people's lives is a community that lives and shares its reality in practice.

The Protestant Reformation peeled back the weight of a

Roman Catholicism that seemed to make salvation a human burden. The crushing expectation of obedience, allegiance, compliance and submission to the code of St. Peter's Basilica in Rome overwhelmed Martin Luther. The stunning, life-giving hope brought about by what Jesus Christ did for us and what we couldn't do for ourselves was expressed in Luther's *sola gratia*. We can be saved by grace alone and never by our capacity to perform and measure up. This rocked Luther's life and the lives of millions since.

Luther pushed this theme adamantly enough that he later concluded that the New Testament book of James was straw because of its insistence that we must act our faith for it to be real. This pushed the pendulum in various Protestant move-ments in a direction that implied faith trumps and diminishes action. It's never about what we do but about what Jesus Christ has done.

This is a reductionist view of Luther, in fact, but it seems to be a pervasive theme in populist Protestantism in the United States. If grace is the only means of eternal salvation, and eternal salvation is all that matters, ordinary action in the ma-terial world falls off the priority list. The paradigm then be-comes that what we do with our days, our bodies and our choices matters, but much less than our faith. Practicing faith becomes an inward and private spiritual exercise, not an outward and public one. We become those who build their houses on sand, not on rock, without even realizing it (Matthew 7:24-28). In fact, it seems we have excised that text from Matthew 7 in favor of simply believing.

GOD'S CALL—DO WE BELIEVE IT OR LIVE IT?

I was at a wedding rehearsal dinner not long ago, chatting with guests of the wedding I would be performing the next day. One young couple I'd just met and who did not know me at all plunged into a surprisingly detailed conversation with me about their relationship, their preferred substance abuse and their highly sexualized life. Suddenly, they asked me what my job was. This is one of those priceless moments for a pastor. I explained who I was and that I was there to perform the wedding the next day. Shocked but undaunted, and on a dime, they said, "Oh, we have Jesus too! And that's all that really matters, right?"

They were reflecting a common misunderstanding propagated by many churches: belief is the evidence of grace. Every time we say we trust in Christ alone, we take the single action that matters. By doing the only worthy thing we can do (believe), we make it clear that we aren't trusting in ourselves. This very act becomes its own mantra. The effect erodes the value of service, of love, of working out our salvation "with

fear and trembling" (Philippians 2:12), of "discern[ing] what is
the will of God—what is good and acceptable and perfect"
(Romans 12:2).

It's an easy step from here to the inference that this life
matters principally as a test of faith, not for intrinsically
meaningful actions of love and service, and that the sufferings of this age are nothing compared to the blessings of
eternal life. The demonstration of God's love and mercy,
kindness and justice here and now is more decorative than
essential. Therefore, the enactment of justice and mercy is
marginalized or treated as useful only if it is a hook for receiving grace.

Our call is meant to be lived out in a world God made and
for which Jesus died. We give ourselves to hear God's call,
which involves hearing how we go about believing and acting
in real time and space, just as God has created and intends.
What we believe matters, but it is evident by how we live.

"The Bible just said so much about the poor, the widow,
the orphan. It just seemed clear to me that this really mattered to God and mattered to me too." This was Jane's
summary of what began as a basic conviction as a new
Christian, and eventually it directed her life work. She had
other plans academically and professionally, but in her
senior year of college, she changed her major and gave

herself to the issues of the urban poor. When Jane was dating the man who would become her husband, she made it clear that if they were to get married, he needed to know she intended to live in the inner city. They did exactly that, including a season in a tiny, one-bedroom apartment in Washington, D.C., where they invited a crack mom and her baby to live with them.

Later Jane and her husband accepted a new opportunity to work for a global foundation caring for the needs of the poor, resulting in a crosscountry move and a new home in the suburbs. That's where they've lived since, and they joke about the moment when Jane so adamantly announced that they would live in the inner city. Her call to live out God's love for the poor is the same, but it has been reframed over time. Out of humility and for fear of overconfidence, Jane would probably not say her work is her "call." And although it has not always looked the way she'd imagined it, she has sought to live what she believes.

Jesus does not say, "Believe me," but rather, "Follow me." If we are going to pursue God's call, it's an act of trusting and following—of behaving and living in ways that reflect our life and purposes. We aren't saved by our actions, but we are saved for our actions to become those that make God's life in Jesus Christ visible.

How Do We Show God's Call?

Rob is a man of faith and a man of science. Though he was
inclined to pursue medicine (for a mix of noble and less-noble
reasons, he admits), he turned instead toward theological and
biblical training. After six great years of youth ministry and a
completed seminary degree, he had finished what he calls
"the most fulfilling part of my life." But continuing to follow
Christ and feeling a hunger to return to science, Rob went off
in the direction of high-risk medical development. It was the
convergence of his personality, his gifts, his opportunities and
his community. Internally, it was a compelling call. Externally,
it was an opportunity to serve humanity and to attend to
some medical needs.

Frederick Buechner says, "The place God calls you to is the
place where your deep gladness and the world's deep hunger
meet."[1] That can often be true. Call can and does emerge from
the inside and the outside of our lives. But for it to be God's
call, it must land in real time and in real space. Rob's double
call to faith and to science converges for him in both domains:
his faith informs and motivates his work in science, and
science speaks to and interacts with his faith. Each has an
authority that rightly fits it, and God holds it all. Rob's experience illustrates that our call comes from the God who holds
"all things . . . together" (Colossians 1:17). It's a life of faith and

a life of action; it's the fruit of what we believe and the evidence of faith being lived.

Scripture says that God, unlike human beings, looks on the heart. When Scripture also says that David most distinguishes himself not as a warrior, king or friend but as one who the Lord says is "a man after my heart" (Acts 13:22), the symmetry captures us. Here is a portrait of divine friendship and intimacy. Here is an anticipation of what Jesus prays for his disciples in John 17: that just as the Father and the Son are one, so we might be one with the Father and the Son by the Spirit.

This, we understand, is a spiritual communion of the heart. It's the only way we could imagine such divine fellowship, and it makes plowing the field, commuting to work, organizing a food drive or playing baseball seem tertiary to the inner work of fellowship with God.

Prayer, then, is the engine. This means cultivating a living conversation with God in all times and places in the face of all the surrounding challenges. Being in a living conversation with God, being a person who lives a life of prayer, is a vital part of our spiritual maturity and a key to discerning God's guidance.

However, some assumptions about spiritual practice make the material world the enemy of the spiritual. Since the rise of gnosticism in the second century, there has been a shadow influence on Christian spirituality. Gnosticism prioritizes the spiritual over and against the material. This idea has an allure because it suggests relief from the burden of daily physical life with all its problems and difficulties. It seems to be a call to purity and away from compromise and ambiguity.

Gnosticism is false, but even so, it is attractive: the inner life is with and for God, and the outer life is distraction. This isn't the reality made known in the incarnation, life, death and resurrection of our Lord. And it isn't the call for the people of God. Jesus' followers are not spiritual escapists. We are instead to be the tangible, material demonstration of the presence, love and justice of God in the physical world that God is renewing.

When seeking to heed God's call, we can't separate the inner from the outer life. This involves unraveling some of the half-truths that can distort our sense of God's call. The assumption seems to be that our inner life is intimate and accessible and personal, and the outer life is pedantic, mechanical and superficial. The assumption is that our inner self is our real self, and our outer self is less so. The inference is that God sees inside us what is both more valuable and more telling. To know someone truly, it goes, we must know something of their heart.

This seems intuitively true. Unfortunately, it's only part of the story. God knows our hearts, yet God also knows our actions. God sees what anyone else might, but God also sees beyond the obvious to the heart. The difference is that God perceives what is hidden; God sees that our hearts are both better and worse than our actions might suggest.

King David's heart both loved better and deceived more than his actions revealed. God sees the whole story, and it's the whole story that matters. So David's cruelty and seduction matter to God—period. And they matter because what was there in David's actions was also there in his heart. His love of God was more authentic and influential than his actions alone could demonstrate. He was suitable for God's call in both his inner and his outer life, though neither was sufficient in itself and neither alone told the whole story.

So instead of this matter with King David driving us to see the whole, we gave the inner life the trump card. This is attractive for various philosophical and psychological reasons, but it's also very pragmatic as an escape route from the weight of actions that don't measure up. We can and do hide in our hearts, relieving ourselves of the burden of falling short, of failing to do what we could have done—or of doing what we did. If we just claim a better, truer heart, it quiets the harassing noise of guilt.

This priority on the heart allows us to believe that if we feel care in our hearts, we are caring. This is convenient but wrong. Care includes our hearts, but it needs to show up in flesh and blood, time and energy. No spouse, child or friend is convinced we care if we don't behave that way. Neither does God. It may be that God sees that we want to care or at least that we know we should care. However, God also knows that our heart's needs subvert our care for other hearts' needs, and caring action is stopped in its tracks.

The inverse of all this can be true as well: we can hide our bitterness or hatred or disregard in our hearts, thinking we are getting away with it, because no one sees but God, and God understands and forgives. This allows our hearts to trump actions too—we can have it both ways. This is often where prejudice, racism, bitterness and pride lurk. We tell ourselves we can love and not have to change. Or we can know in our hearts that we hate but never be exposed or transformed.

John knows what lurks in his heart and life. He has a keen awareness of the issues within, some of which have nearly swamped him. His professional life involves endless, aggressive negotiations. But now the grace of God has called him to follow Jesus, and the difference can be seen. In all honesty and candor before God, John is in the process of dealing with his underlying issues. Things have gradually turned in his life because of his sense of call. This means he now consciously embraces the opponent in a negotiation to be the one God is most calling him to engage and love in the coming year. As this has been happening, it is showing up in dramatically changed relationships and business dealings. John's is a story of what's happening inside and out.

Ken grew up in a devout pastor's home—he was a pastor's kid in an activist, urban ministry setting. Personal faith and action were one. His heart was for Christ to transform cities. Though he sensed God might be calling him to pastoral ministry, he was more interested in serving the world through some kind of social change involving engineering and science. This brought him to the study of engineering and a career of public service, building roads and bridges that shape the lives of ordinary people and neighborhoods every day. This has been his way of knitting the inner and outer life together. Faith in action is his daily mantra. He has sought to live his faith tangibly by loving people with the right bridge, in the right place, through the right process. Ken said, "I think God took my desire to go in this direction, which may not have been God's first desire for me, and honored it. What started as my own inner desire became my call to do this public service."

In God's full knowledge of us, both the inner and the outer life matter. Our practices of faith are meant to show up in both domains and to become a mutual validation of each other. This is what it means to reflect the glory of God—the reality of God—whose heart and actions are congruent. But this isn't our nature, which is why we need grace. The work of grace is to move us to become people whose inner and outer lives bear witness to the mercy and truth of God's love and justice—made whole, healed and renewed. If you are "transformed by the renewing of your minds," it is so that you can "discern what is the will of God—what is good and acceptable and perfect"—and that happens in real time (Romans 12:2).

PRACTICE

Invite a trusted friend or family member to spend time helping you identify the ways in which you are not only "believing" but also "following."

- Before your visit, prayerfully consider what specific ways you believe God may be calling you to "follow" in your day-to-day interactions. Invite the Holy Spirit to help you remain open to assessing honestly how well you are following, not just believing.

- Share these thoughts with your friend and invite reflection on the ways in which you're already living this call and the ways in which your actions may not be as evident as you had hoped.

- Make a plan with your friend of ways in which you can help encourage each other in your faithful actions.

6

REFOCUSING

To Whom and to What Are We Called?

Another thing we have to unravel about call is whether it's first and foremost a private call. Is it about me or about us? Who receives God's call?

Bowling Alone is the title of Robert Putnam's 2000 bestseller (subtitled *The Collapse and Revival of American Community*). It explores the increasing social void many experience, the emptiness many people feel in relation to others. It is sobering. A lot of things have happened in the last dozen years since its publication, including 9/11, the explosion of social media and the 2008 global economic meltdown. When put together, the picture of our social relations—near and far, up and down the economic ladder, around the world, across racial and religious lines—adds up to social division and personal isolation apparently having increased and decreased at the same time.

Some of the most common lost practices in our daily lives have to do with community. One of the ironies of an increasingly urbanized world and a global population of more than seven billion is that people commonly experience life alone. We're ever nearer physically, but we're also ever more isolated from one another. Putnam shows that over the last twenty-five years, attendance at club meetings has dropped 58 percent, family dinners have dropped 43 percent and having friends over has dropped by 35 percent.[1] We crave community even as we seek to avoid it.

Community should be a natural cornerstone of life as a Christian disciple; we're meant to be a part of the community of God's people. After all, Christian disciples can't live faithfully by themselves, and we seldom hear the call of God alone. Biblically, the call of God is inextricable from the community of God's people, yet the church in the United States is rife with evidence that the church seeks and avoids community, just like the culture around it. This varies based on denomination and region of the country, but it's hard to stand against a culture that prioritizes the individual and encourages every individual to do likewise. That is the trap.

It's also hard for a disparate group of busy people, who commute varying distances to worship, whose lives do not intersect in daily activities and whose places of play and relaxation aren't the same, to make one another a priority. Efforts can and are made to compensate for this at many churches, but it can be difficult. Add to this the increasing number of multiethnic congregations in which growing in love and support across social boundaries of race and ethnicity can be daunting. When our primary patterns reinforce staying in our own social group, it seems improbable that church community can occupy enough time and space to produce real change.

Central Christian Church in Phoenix is a booming church that wants to move directly against the sort of consumer Christianity that indulges the appetites of the individual above all else. When people are baptized in their church, they are given a T-shirt with the words "Made for more than just me." That's the kind of identity the church needs to recover, and it's fundamental to a biblical view of call.

With Whom Are We Called?

We are born into a sociological baseline of division from one another. In some cases, these are deep and passionate lines of distinction, perhaps ethnic, economic or religious. Even when they are less contentious, everyone recognizes their reality and encounters their implications. It's the stuff of tribe or nation, neighborhood or family. Resentment and aggression are pervasive. Violence and warfare seem natural. Even the rivalry of athletic teams shows the marks of this legacy. All this forms the personal or public environment in which we grow up and in relation to which we emerge as adults, generation after generation.

Into just such a world comes Jesus, who "will save his people from their sins" (Matthew 1:21). He lives and loves so that his people "may be one, as we [he and the Father] are one" (John 17:11). For in his death on the cross, he "has broken down the dividing wall, that is, the hostility between us" and created one new humanity (Ephesians 2:14). This is the new sociology of the people of God.

And yet the story doesn't play out the way Jesus intended, and our clinging to old divisions—inside and outside the people of God—seems normative. Instead of the unity meant to characterize us, we have a scandal of perpetual division.

We fail again and again in practicing our identity. The divisions can benignly appear in jokes ("A Baptist, a Presbyterian and a Roman Catholic went into a bar . . .") and seem almost endearing. But they can also lead to disdain and even bloodshed.

God's people are redeemed and loved into a new world and are meant to enact this toward one another. "By this everyone will know that you are my disciples, if you have love for one another" (John 13:35). This is not assumed to be easy or natural—that isn't the point. It's a daunting life to try to live, and we do it by faith, seeking God's transforming love all along the way. "If you love those who love you, what credit is that to you? For even sinners love those who love them" (Luke 6:32). That is a serious practice that's beyond us and can be learned only in action.

Jesus decides who our fellow disciples will be, and from all evidence of the New Testament, it will be an unlikely set of relationships. If our experience of Christian community is simply the sociology we would have anyway, apart from Christ, with no evidence that we're called beyond ourselves and into a new community, we have good reason to ask whether we're hearing and following God's call. All the evidence of the New Testament is that the new humanity into which we're baptized is meant to look like the unexpected, varied community of those who admit their need and seek Jesus as Savior and Lord.

On our good days, we settle for connection with others when deep communion demands too much. Rather than aim our practice toward sharing with at least some people at the deepest of levels, we choose the bland path of mere connection.

This is ideal in a social-media-driven world. Our hunger

may be for something more profound, but contact can be a social palliative and doesn't require the complications of time, energy and vulnerability that communion requires. For many, these cyberspace interactions are real points of contact. They may even involve some degree of intimacy, and they keep things moving and flowing, flexible and changeable. This feels adaptive, which simply means the relationships can be dropped when they're less desirable or serviceable, so little damage or fallout is involved.

Being near someone is easier than knowing them or being known by them. In relationships of communion, where we weep together and rejoice together, where we live as members one of another, where we are each part of one common body in Christ, much more is required than mere contact or connection. Stepping into one another's lives, listening and hearing one another's stories, honoring one another's unique gifts, carrying one another's burdens—this is the stuff of community.

Connecting can skate on the surface of this and may intersect with it at times. In fact, communion typically begins at this level and moves deeper. But if connecting is taken as the limit and not just the beginning, what is found is far less than what is there to be discovered.

When the church mimics the culture in these relational patterns, we surrender our call. Megachurches symbolically lead in the image of the church-industrial complex. Much good can and does go on in such contexts, but the stereotype image is one of "connecting" more than of dwelling or communing together. The same can also be true of the small neighborhood church that is all about form and association but not true communion with one another.

We may long to know others and to be known, but the subculture teaches us to practice superficiality rather than honesty, to share competencies, not weaknesses, and to hide skillfully rather than seek genuine trust. That doesn't work for any generation, but especially for young adults and younger.

In a connection society, we're happier experiencing diversity from a distance than we are in close interdependence. We prefer the idea of proximity to difference more than actually entering into friendship with people unlike us. We love humanity; it's people we don't like.

My wife and I now live in the Los Angeles area. Endless cultural and ethnic variation surrounds us. But when I ask people of different ethnic backgrounds whether they're good friends with anyone who doesn't share their ethnic heritage, it's unusual for them to say yes. They experience proximate diversity but not intimate diversity.

Many factors contribute to this, some of which have already been described. The net implication, however, is that we are prone to stay in our silos rather than to experience the risk and joy of a life intertwined with someone who is truly not like us in ethnicity, background, personality or in other ways.

The love that's meant to be the essential characteristic of God's people is a love that surprises. It embodies genuine boundary-crossing care, unexplained by expectations or categories such as class or race and earned through reciprocity. It isn't about pretending we can or should live in a "color-free" society, as though social differences don't exist. That's idealism, not compassionate, humble realism. That's a romanticized vision of love, not the gritty, incarnational love our Lord exemplifies and calls us to demonstrate.

When the church's characteristics simply look like a baptized version of the sociology we would live if we weren't disciples, we're failing to practice the love that demonstrates the new reality into which we are baptized in Christ. Without that reality, talk of diversity becomes an aesthetics lecture, not a vivid enactment of the kingdom. We are called to live our vocation.

One of the most important effects of the gospel in my own life has been the way it has enlarged my sociology. Through being a student at Fuller Seminary, with more than one hundred nations in the student body, through several decades of being involved in international ministries and through close friendships with pastors and leaders in various places I have lived, my world has grown and changed. The most important ways have been through knowing individuals who have been honest enough to let me in on their lives and their worlds, which were not like my own. I'm forever changed by friendships that have given me different eyes for my neighbor and greater love in response.

To What Are We Called?

I couldn't tell you how many times I've had conversations with people seeking God's will, trying to hear God's call on their lives. For a thoughtful and deliberate disciple, this seeking is natural and compelling. It may be approached with a sense of urgency (such as when about to graduate from college with no plans) or in the midst of transitions (such as when changing jobs or making a critical decision) or in the midst of great pain (such as when caring for parents or children, or grieving a loss). We need to be sure about what we're seeking and to what end we're seeking it. That is why I find it helpful to distinguish "first things" from "next things."

First things. If what we're seeking is God's will and call on our lives, the most substantial dimensions of that are already revealed in Scripture, and especially in Jesus Christ. These are the first things that are normative for those who follow as disciples. They are matters of character and of faith, of obedience and of influence, of priorities. God's call is that we love God first and our neighbors second and that, by the power of the Holy Spirit, we come to bear the fruit of the Spirit in our lives: "love, joy, peace, patience, kindness, generosity, faithfulness, gentleness, and self-control" (Galatians 5:22-23).

Without any special guidance from the Holy Spirit, with no anxiety or worry, and with utter confidence, we can daily pursue these first things as our primary vocation. We'll explore all of this later in this book (and, in fact, much more in a subsequent book).

Next things. Beyond these first things, God sometimes has next things. These aspects of our call assume first things but then move us in particular contexts of work or ministry, of friendship or marriage, of service or advocacy, of imagination or analysis. These next things may take the form of jobs (and often do), or they may be acts of volunteer service. This is where the convergence of gifts, talents, education, opportunity, passion and more draw us toward jobs or service that can seem deeply rewarding.

Next things are not first things, nor vice versa, even though both matter and they're tied together. This is what Daniel and his friends in Babylon demonstrated so well. The first thing was that they belonged to Yahweh even when they lived in

Nebuchadnezzar's house. The second was that they could carry out next things with clarity of vision and resolve that meant they could even face fire with freedom (Daniel 3).

What matters, at the moment, is to be truly and fully clear that the call of the first things is primary. Yet the temptation is to make the next things first things. This is a classic tangle and fails to give full weight to what really matters most. So we go to work and forget or neglect who we are, what our life is really about, how we seek to love and serve. We enter the subculture of our activities, and soon that reality begins to define and shape us, rather than the other way around.

We are meant to pursue and develop *first things* as we go about *next things;* we do this simultaneously, remembering that first and next things are not the same. In Scripture, God seems far more passionate about first things—how we live and love him and our neighbor—than about next things—what our set of daily tasks is. At the same time, it's clear how we love him and our neighbor by how we demonstrate that in the context of our daily relationships and tasks. This is where the ordinary joy and rub of Christian discipleship are meant to be lived out. We live out the extraordinary call of following Jesus (first things) right in the midst of the ordinary actions of daily life (next things).

Called to Lead

When some hear the word *lead* or *leadership*, they immediately step up, while others immediately step back. Both actions can be forms of leadership, and any true disciple is in some measure meant to be a leader—one who affects others by the way he or she lives, acts and speaks. Jesus-following leaders are needed everywhere.

All over the world, leaders are in crisis. At a time of extraordinary local and global change, any leader paying attention knows that things are not like they have been and won't be like we have imagined. What things will be like, however, will be an expression of leadership, even though most leaders have little or no idea where to go or how to lead in such a time as this.

The speed and scale of changes, the randomness of social media's impact and the relentlessness of invisible technological system-makers and system-busters leave many with a sense of free fall. Then you add the chronic problems of injustice, poverty and violence that undermine daily life for much of the world's population, and it all seems overwhelming. "Do something!" might be the instinctive cry. But how? In what way? To what end? Such questions have few immediate clear answers.

Hence the need for leaders. Today more than ever, leadership isn't first and foremost a formal role. It's rather a personal capacity to exert vision and passion that enables others to join in a common effort. Such leaders are needed in every domain of life. They don't hold the resolution; they hold the capacity to draw others into seeking and working toward one. They may have a title and job description, or they may simply be influencers.

We may or may not think of ourselves as leaders. Perhaps no title or role tells us or anyone else we are leaders. But those reading this book have the opportunities and the capacity—in fact, the Christian responsibility—to influence the world around us. The leadership gap is then not just a word for "them" but a word for all of us.

Leaders with vision are more than people with hope. Many have hope, but few have vision. Vision is hope with commitment and energy. The church in exile needs those who have vision grounded in the hope of the grace and love of Jesus Christ, who are gripped by a clear engagement with the world around us, who are drawn together with other followers and who are ready to exercise transformational leadership.

Such impact can come through institutional or personal initiative. It can be found when parents band with teachers to change a neighborhood school. It is evident when a person's medical crisis is championed by a friend who leads others to rally in her support throughout her treatment. It's seen when a peace-making leader confronts racial hatred in a city by inviting people of goodwill and compassion to do something about it. It comes to the fore when someone begins to see and care about human trafficking or violence against the poor and invites others to join him in doing something to make a difference. Not all of these roles have titles, but all of them involve leadership.

In the church that finds itself in exilic times, it would be easy to think exile means impotence and the loss of a capacity to bring change or influence. Nothing could be further from the truth! In fact, the Bible shows exilic leaders doing just what exile itself distinctly creates the opportunity to do.

In the Old Testament, Daniel and his friends are depicted as exiles who are given special privilege in Nebuchadnezzar's house—a classic assimilation effort of the vanquished by the vanquisher. Time and again, however, Daniel and the others demonstrate a readiness to lead—and to do so not just for their own survival or benefit but also for the sake of their rivals and oppressors.

Daniel and his cohort led and made a difference because they had hope in God's capacity for change, combined with their own commitment to serve and engage. They rehearsed and practiced their identity as children of Yahweh every time they ate (Daniel 1). They stepped up and into the challenges they were presented with and did so for the sake of their enemies as well as for themselves (Daniel 2). They kept themselves clear about issues of power. They weren't hooked by Nebuchadnezzar's rage. They knew his anxious request was beyond their own capacity but not beyond their God. They stood together in prayer and sought God's answer.

They received from God what was bad and terrifying news for Nebuchadnezzar, but they brought it to him without condition and with boldness. It was a dream about the dissolution of his own powerful kingdom, yet Nebuchadnezzar heard and received it as good and impressive news because it confirmed what he had believed was the truth (Daniel 2). Four exiles led the most powerful man in the world to see the end of his own supremacy and to hear about the God who alone raises up and brings down rulers. Even the rage that threatened to consume them when they refused to worship an idol did not control them. They lived free and unhooked lives: "O Nebuchadnezzar, we have no need to present a defense to you in this matter" (Daniel 3:16). Die or live, they would not bow down and worship a false god. Nebuchadnezzar had power; they had leadership.

In Scripture, the supreme example of this is, of course, Jesus. He was clearly an exilic leader. As one without stature or role, whose life was lived with those at the margins, Jesus led. His hope-filled vision of the kingdom invited his disciples to join in the commitment and energy of faith needed to seek God's provision of a new creation.

What unfolds from Jesus' influence is without peer, and it's in a context in which Israel, let alone Jesus' followers, felt like hopeless exiles without power or authority. Jesus led through the cross and beyond to enact in unique terms the beginning of a new reality right in the midst of the old and lost one.

This reframing of reality is the cornerstone of Christian leadership. In Matthew 28, the text makes it clear that the risen Jesus gathered with only eleven disciples (not twelve, as first asked) who both believe and doubt (not undoubting believers!) (see Matthew 28:16-17). And to these few believer-doubters, Jesus handed nothing less than the authority of the kingdom. He charged them to go forth and lead that kingdom life, baptizing them (a new identity) and teaching them all he commanded (a new vocation) and promising to be with them "to the end of the age" (Matthew 28:20).

This is the most unexpected and enormously encouraging vision of leadership anywhere. For all the church's failures and struggles, its deceit and its brokenness, its tedium and its distractions, Jesus has used the church in the world to accomplish many great ends by the Spirit. As far short as the church has often fallen, and that is very far indeed, God's willingness and faithfulness to use the few and vulnerable to change the world remains.

The church, like Israel, keeps thinking it has to win and be the victor in order to have the power. Since the fourth century, when Constantine legalized Christianity in the Roman Empire, the church in the Western world has aligned itself with power. The truth, however, is that God doesn't need that authority or power to accomplish kingdom ends. What's needed instead is a readiness to live our vocation centered on the One who alone gives us our identity and our hope.

> So if you have been raised with Christ, seek the things that are above, where Christ is, seated at the right hand of God. Set your minds on things that are above, not on things that are on earth, for you have died, and your life is hidden with Christ in God. When Christ who is your life is revealed, then you also will be revealed with him in glory. (Colossians 3:1-4)

WISE LEADERS

In sum, our vocation involves becoming wise leaders. Biblical wisdom is

> the truth and character of God
> lived
> in context.

When all three of those elements converge, we have the makings of wisdom. When any of them is lacking, we have the beginnings of folly. Our vocation is found in the process of seeking the kingdom, letting it shape how we actually live and doing so in ever-changing contexts. To do this in the Promised Land is one thing. To do it in exile is quite another. By doing so at all, we become leaders in many and varied ways, since this is the catalyst for change and re-creation.

These three dimensions of biblical wisdom are like an intertwined spiral, each pushing on and affecting the others. When this unfolds in the context of the beloved community, with the chance to exercise the commitments and gifts God has given us with faith and hope and love, God's people act as salt and light. We begin to live our vocation as shining stars (Philippians 2:15).

The church doesn't need chaplains for a church in Christendom. It urgently needs those who flourish in exile because they are following Jesus, not their dreams of the Promised Land.

PRACTICE

Memorize all nine of the fruit of the Spirit: love, joy, peace, patience, kindness, generosity, faithfulness, gentleness and self-control. Spend a few days reciting them often and incorporating them into your prayer life. Consider which of these are most evident in your life and which less so.

- Choose one specific fruit of the Spirit you feel led to embody more fully.

- Create a reminder that represents this characteristic in some way and can encourage its development. For example,

  - an object to carry in your pocket or handbag;

  - an alert that goes off periodically on your phone or calendar;

  - notes to post on your mirror, on your refrigerator, in your car or elsewhere; or

  - a song to play each morning and evening, or during your commute.

- Pay attention to cues that may help you recognize your progress. Invite trusted friends or colleagues to share observations that may be helpful.

7

THE WAY OF
THE BELOVED

A man once appeared at my office door, and in so many words, he said, "I'm very busy and very successful and don't really have time for this, but I wonder if we could talk for five minutes."

"By all means," I said.

"Well," he went on, "my wife has been attending this church and now at dinner she's talking about Jesus, and I don't know anything about Jesus, so I thought I'd come by for a few bullet points about Jesus."

"Wow, I'm not sure I can help you. For one thing, I'm not good with bullet points, and for another, even if I could give you some good bullet points about Jesus, I'm afraid it could have a way of getting into your life that would cause you to rethink your power and your success and your money and your marriage and your family—everything."

"Oh, I don't want to do that. Not at all! I just want some bullet points about Jesus."

"How about changing the subject at dinner?" I offered.

Following Jesus changes everything. We start with first things—the things most easily overlooked in busy lives.

THE FIRST OF FIRST THINGS

We start recovering our call when we learn which first things are first. The love of God in Jesus Christ is the supreme first thing; no one and nothing rivals or surpasses this. If we want to know ourselves and why our life matters, the Bible's advice is to know our Maker, who knows and loves us fully.

This is, of course, why Christians believe that coming to faith in Jesus Christ matters so much—not because it's like handing out a "get into heaven free" card, but because it's like offering an invitation to know yourself through the love of God in Jesus Christ, a gift that will change how you understand your identity and therefore how you live both now and in eternity. Knowing ourselves and knowing God are inseparable.[1]

If we try to settle the issues of calling through the lens of our strengths and weaknesses, our preferences and dreams, we will be prone to overreach (because we make ourselves and our desires the ultimate measure) or underreach (because we're willing to allow ourselves or someone other than God to tell us who we are). Over the course of our lives, neither works well or leads us to the truth.

We matter, and our calling matters, not because we're the supreme test of anything but because we exist for the joy and satisfaction of our Maker, whose love alone enables us to flourish. Here is the context in which we come to see ourselves as "fearfully and wonderfully made" by the One who "knit [us] together in [our] mother's womb" (Psalm 139:13-14). Our vocation will involve work and labor, and that has its meaning and value. But we are "very good" in God's sight because of bearing God's image—not because we are fruitful and multiply (Genesis 1:28) but just because we are.

Our first vocation is to be the beloved. The primacy of God's unearned love alone makes this possible. We live as the beloved, the treasured. This vocation is pure gift. Whatever the human context or circumstances surrounding our birth, our life is a cherished gift to be signed with God's love. This is the vocation of living as a beloved one. To live into this and to allow this to frame and to hold us in all our days is to live into our first thing.

If we're fortunate, we grow up in a context in which this affirmation of being beloved by God is formative from the start. Before school or soccer or ballet was even in sight, let alone graduation or our first job, we may have come to know how God and our family treasure us.

If this message has been consistently affirmed and enacted in your life, you are among the fortunate. For many, neither family nor God landed this way in their psychology or identity—maybe just the opposite, in fact. Neglect, addiction, abuse distort our lives. "But God, who is rich in mercy" (Ephesians 2:4), has another plan and welcomes us to live and walk in this new life.

This affirmation of our belovedness arises not as a derivative of belief about an abstractly benevolent deity but rather in trusting God's tangible care. This has been Israel's solid hope: "Now thus says the LORD, he who created you, O Jacob, he who formed you, O Israel: Do not fear, for I have redeemed you; I have called you by name, you are mine" (Isaiah 43:1). Now that affirmation has been clothed with incarnate evidence in Emmanuel, God with us, Jesus. The fact that "God so loved the world that he gave his only Son, so that everyone who believes in him may not perish but may have eternal life" bears witness to our belovedness (John 3:16).

We are to live Paul's advice:

Let the same mind be in you that was in Christ Jesus,
 who, though he was in the form of God,
  did not regard equality with God
  as something to be exploited,
 but emptied himself,
  taking the form of a slave,
  being born in human likeness.
 And being found in human form,
  he humbled himself
  and became obedient to the point of death—
  even death on a cross.

 Therefore God also highly exalted him
  and gave him the name
  that is above every name,
 so that at the name of Jesus
  every knee should bend,
  in heaven and on earth and under the earth,
 and every tongue should confess
  that Jesus Christ is Lord,
  to the glory of God the Father. (Philippians 2:5-11)

The first of first things in our vocation is this relationship of first importance. It enlarges and releases all else. The watering, nurturing, tending, pruning, shepherding, feeding, watchful, sacrificing, redeeming Son of God longs for us to receive our belovedness:

> Come to me, all you that are weary and are carrying heavy burdens, and I will give you rest. Take my yoke upon you, and learn from me; for I am gentle and humble in heart, and you will find rest for your souls. For my yoke is easy, and my burden is light. (Matthew 11:28-30)

The love of God is the start and the finish of our vocation.

BELOVED TOGETHER

We are to live as the beloved together—with other human beings but with those in Christ's family especially. We are the conglomeration of the unexpected. We are the recipients of the down payment of the kingdom of God by the indwelling Holy Spirit. All this becomes the makings of "one new humanity" (Ephesians 2:15), the beloved community.

My vocation can be discovered only in the context of *our* vocation. It only makes sense that it would be so, since belovedness is never isolated or singular. We discover and live our belovedness in Christ with and for one another. This is what church means.

Being part of the *ecclesia*—the called ones—means practicing this identity of belovedness together. We declare it and remind each other of it. We rehearse it when we share in the sacraments of baptism and the Lord's Supper. Each embodies the affirmation of how tangible and real God's loving engagement with us and with our world has been and is still to be. Baptism declares that our belovedness is a settled identity. It is a bedrock affirmation. The communion table enables us to go on doing this "in remembrance of him" because we go on needing to receive and to share this love repeatedly. Here we are again, at the table, receiving and sharing who we are and why we are.

We come to the table out of need, because our belovedness is slippery. It can fall through our fingers or leave our minds. But when we gather to eat and drink, we enact our identity and we practice remembering Jesus' love, and that regrounds us in the first things about today and every day. Whatever job we may have in the workplace or at home, whatever neighbors we may be trying to love, whatever heartache or need we may be facing, we remember ourselves by remembering Jesus Christ. We come to the table together and leave together, remembering that our vocation starts and ends as the beloved community.

Of course, this is easier said than done, and that's why our doing it over and over is so important. We come in frailty and in joy. We come at times when being loved and loving are anything but clear or natural. We come in hope and also in brokenness. We come full-hearted and we come empty-handed. We come loving one another, but we also come in our division, in our resentment of or boredom with one another. Every time, like hitting a reset button, we remember Jesus said, "This is my body, which is given for you. Do this in remembrance of me. . . . This cup that is poured out for you is the new covenant in my blood" (Luke 22:19-20).

If we're fortunate, we hear these words in a group of like and unlike folks. We look across the table and see those whose faces tell different stories than our own. Their skin tone, their clothing, their age, their posture, their eyes invite us into a communion we didn't make and can't sustain. We sit or kneel as we do so, receiving the common gift of God's grace in this simple meal. As we do so, we're practicing why we are alive and what we are to do.

Life in the beloved community is often more broken than healed, more confusing than clear, more divided than one—but it is of the very essence of our identity and vocation. We live as the beloved, and we rehearse what that means in the communion of others who share it. It's a space where we can get some things marvelously, wonderfully right. We can also do injury. No one said it would be perfect. But Jesus said it would be an easy yoke and a light burden (Matthew 11:30). It's the right work, even if it's tough.

Few things make us need the gospel more than the experience of the church. We may lean into our belovedness readily, until we realize it involves doing so with others. The saying "I love humanity; it's people that are the problem" could have been written because of the church. The very difficulties and challenges are right before us. We may decide to bail from a given church or community, but in the end we discover that living in the new setting, in the new beloved community, will once again be a calling that will require more than we have. That's why we must keep remembering and keep practicing our vocation of belovedness for our sake and for the sake of our beloved community.

The Freedom to Make First Things Primary

A big gap yawns between our values and our actions. We may believe in the importance of something but not allow it to affect our lives all that much. Family or friends may be our highest value, but it can be hard to prove that by looking at how we spend our time. Or we may claim that issues of justice are supremely important to us, and yet our resources never quite get directed toward making a difference. We all know this disconnection about ourselves. We get distracted by the thing that's fifteenth or thirty-second on our list and fail to do what we claim is first.

What we need is the freedom to make what's first primary. If—and this is the point of uncertainty—we can live out of our true belovedness and do so with others, we can begin to live out the values we affirm. This is itself a critical ingredient in living our vocation. It's not about how to squeeze in one more commitment. It's about reframing everything in light of what we consider of first importance.

This takes freedom. When Israel became captive to Babylon, and Daniel and others among the best and brightest were taken to live in Nebuchadnezzar's house, everything they held of first importance was taken from them. As these young men were forced to live in a new context with new names and a new language, assimilation was the empire's goal. Yet Daniel and his friends did something profound: they asked for the freedom to maintain the dietary laws of their people. Every time they ate, they were quietly making what was first primary: they lived in Nebuchadnezzar's house but they belonged to Yahweh (Daniel 1–3). Everything is changed. This is the critical step. What unfolds from there affects the rest of their story.

This same pattern is behind the apostle Paul's exhortation in Romans, "I appeal to you therefore, brothers and sisters, by the mercies of God, to present your bodies as a living sacrifice, holy and acceptable to God, which is your spiritual worship" (Romans 12:1). If we allow what is first to become primary in our lives, the rest begins to take shape. We start living the vocation for which we are made.

Augustine described sin as disordered love. We have been made to love God first, but then we try to satisfy that love by loving ourselves first instead. Satisfaction eludes us, and the downward spiral of self-absorption undermines our lives. But if we live into the freedom of God's grace, we begin to take up our vocation: we are made to live out of God's belovedness first and primarily. When that occurs, we have a far, far greater likelihood of coming to all else in our lives with more capacity to live and to love.

Jesus demonstrated again and again a life that makes what is first primary. It didn't involve a form of legalism; it was an expression of freedom and clarity. To live the Sermon on the Mount is to live a reordered life. We approach relationships of power and struggle differently. We find understanding rather than anger. We realize that words matter more than we thought. We see that our inner life and our outer life are meant to be one thing. We reconsider what love means, not just toward those who love us but even more toward those who are our enemies. And in all this, if we make what is first primary, we live differently.

When, like Jesus, we come down from the mountain and encounter a leper in need or an oppressor with profound faith, we have a far greater chance of seeing and loving our neighbor than would be true otherwise. This means we live into our vocation in its profound and subversive forms as God's peculiar people, doing what Jesus did in great measure and with deep love.

We start looking like the One we follow.

MAKE WHAT'S PRIMARY PERVASIVE

Living as the beloved and following Jesus together is meant to pervade all that we are and do. This is to be our life. It can and needs to occur throughout all dimensions of our life: heart, mind and strength. It can and needs to pervade all the world. It's meant to show up in all kinds of cultural and workplace settings. It unfolds in neighborhoods, in schools and in art galleries. It happens over the back fence, online and in carpools. It's living Jesus' life in the midst of the ordinary.

Authentic discipleship delivers us from a compartmentalized life. Rather than having a life with segments and partitions—divisions between sacred and secular, personal and public, image and reality—we're called to one whole and integrated life.

It has to be said, of course, that usually we don't want such a life and prefer the separate compartments. Such divisions provide room for our conflicting and contradictory instincts and desires. This is how we try to manage our several selves. It's the hedge-your-bets approach to life, highly appealing but ultimately disappointing. It's like approaching life as a series of snacks rather than committing ourselves to a full meal.

Dissonant fragments make a disciple's life inauthentic. When being a follower of Jesus means having a switch turned on when it's convenient and off when it becomes costly, the life of faith becomes marginalized. This can be felt both by disciples themselves and by those around them. Suddenly, what had seemed robust and healthy fades or collapses. For those who already suspect that faith is a spiritual shell game, this inconsistency seems to be corroborating evidence.

Of course, only Jesus had a fully integrated and fully human life. But this isn't to suggest life is perfection or it's nothing. Not at all! Living a coherent vocation of seeking to follow Jesus leads us toward a vital, humble life of faith, honesty and hope that pervades our lives.

Mike is a fourth-generation Pentecostal with roots that go all the way back to the Azusa Street revival and still-deeper roots that go back into African soil. Raised in the working class with college-educated parents, he grew up in an urban, African American scene and attended a largely white, private, Christian school until high school. Racial dynamics were part of the reason for the change.

What really changed for him, however, began on March 9, 1999. Mike was a youth pastor and was on his way home from the Christian college he attended when the police stopped him for no apparent reason. What ensued was a life-changing set of events. First, he was mugged, handcuffed and then beaten by the police. In the subsequent months, the police denied all of it, leaving Mike and those closest to him deeply disturbed.

Mike had to make peace with this spiritually and emotionally. He said it was like a crossroads, and he had to make sense of the pain and trauma. His bedrock was that he knew he was an African American and a Pentecostal. That was his starting point for beginning to recover and heal. And experiencing all this focused his sense of call. He knew he was called to live as a Christian in response to such a racially troubled context: this was the first thing. But he also felt called as a pastor serving mostly other African American Pentecostals who must live as followers of Jesus in the midst of those realities. His life trajectory was set in motion. His call to live as a follower of Jesus was first and primary, and he gradually allowed his experience to pervade his community and the wider society of which he was a part. He continues this journey today.

To embrace our vocation as Jesus' followers is to pervade our thoughts *and* our actions—not just one or the other. It likewise is to pervade our public as well as our private lives. This happens not as a labeling exercise—such as wearing a support button or being listed as a member of something— but rather as we welcome the transformative inner work of the Holy Spirit. The vocation is the journey of opening ourselves to this deep and deepening work that pervades us as we become new creatures.

Everyone acknowledges the developmental realities of childhood and the teenage years. But when those who claim to be followers of Jesus never seem to get through and beyond those phases to the place of pervading faith and love, something is wrong with the faith or with the person, or with both. If people that grow up in church never seem to grow up in life or in wisdom, that's a problem. When those outside the church get the impression that even the leading public voices of faith are immature or fragmented, they assume this is true of the church at large.

When many outside the church live more integrated, loving lives than some of the church's leaders do, the church's failure to live out its vocation has understandable implications. Some in the church deflect this with the bumper-sticker aphorism "Christians are forgiven, not perfect," but that misses the point. What people are measuring is not perfection but basic consistency and coherence: a competent teacher who truly loves his students; a business owner who is reliably honest; a pastor who faithfully preaches from Scripture and seeks the welfare of her congregation; a parent who consistently decides what to do for the best of his child; a friend who initiates and remembers.

Has the gospel we proclaim and affirm pervaded our lives or not? If no evidence of greater love or deeper humility or greater courage or tangible sacrifice is evident in our lives, why do we think our faith matters even to us, let alone to the world surrounding us? This is the practical and sometimes graphic void that confuses and offends many about the life of the church.

COLLIDING EXPECTATIONS

Following Jesus is no easy path for anyone at any time. It is, however, made even harder when we try to do so as though we live in one place when in fact we live in another. This is the temptation of the Promised Land delusion. If we understand that exile is now home, we embrace and live into our vocation in a far more realistic and constructive way. We may feel wistful for some other context, but we can live much more positively if we grasp the nature of the challenges at hand. The other, the different and the enemy are the "new normal," the gift God gives us for our growth and for our vocation of unexpected love.

The dissonance is intrinsic to the calling rather than the problem itself. As Christendom continues to fade culturally, people who seek to follow Jesus have a new set of expectations. The expectation that the church's voice will be resonant with the voice of the dominant culture must be surrendered. This will increasingly be the case in much of North America.

What's more, the recovery of Christendom is not the goal. The closest the United States has come to this was known as American civil religion, and it was at best a secularized version of public goodness and justice. That is hardly a kingdom dream.

What we need is a recovery of call that knows where we live and how we can live faithfully for the sake of God's kingdom.

Practice

Choose a spiritual practice you can commit to for at least one week. (If you already have a particular spiritual practice, consider trying something new or different during this time.) Use this practice as an opportunity to grow in your vocation as "the beloved."

- Here are some practices you may find helpful:

    - Embrace a traditional practice such as *lectio divina*, fixed hour prayer or *examen* of consciousness. Abundant resources for these and many other spiritual disciplines are available in bookstores and online. Some particular authors you may wish to look for include Ruth Haley Barton, Richard Foster, Phyllis Tickle or Oscar Romero.

- Read or recite a Scripture text, prayer or creed at specific intervals during the day.
- Journal for fifteen minutes each morning or evening.
- Fast from technology by making your household "screen free" for a certain amount of time each day.

- What do you find especially helpful or challenging?
- As the week progresses, do the disciplines become easier or more difficult?
- Has this practice helped you experience God's love more fully? If not, what else might you try?
- What is something you could continue to practice on a long-term basis?

8

THE WAY OF WISDOM

The one thing every Jesus follower needs every day is always the same: wisdom. In other words, we need an understanding of God's vision in action that will make a kingdom difference in people's lives.

God's wisdom isn't just theological insight, of course. To talk about needing wisdom is not to talk about how to live as an armchair sage. Wisdom is not necessarily about more information, even more biblical information.

When I was serving as a pastor, I felt my need for true wisdom, as did all those I encountered. We longed for wisdom in pastoral conversations when someone's capacities for life's challenges ran thin or when decisions were being made. At many a hospital bedside, especially when the diagnosis was threatening, we sought wisdom. It happens too in financial discussions, job searches, ministry decisions. It occurs when walking down the street and being overwhelmed (again) by the complexities of people's lives.

Jesus followers hope that God's wisdom will shape what we say and do, and what in turn others may hear and do. Of course, God's wisdom almost always complicates things by intensifying our life's meaning and enlarging our vocation. If God does speak and is heard, life will be more like it was intended to be. And that, almost surely, won't make life easier.

Rehabilitating Wisdom

Wisdom may or may not be the name used to describe what we seek, but our instincts call for something that is real, active and contextual. Here are some guiding assumptions:

- Wisdom is God's truth and character lived in context. Jesus is God's wisdom. That's who and what wisdom looks like.

- Our world needs wise disciples who form wise communities, who live wisely in the world. That is, in all the local and global dimensions of life and society, our world needs disciples who show up in every aspect and place of life and ministry—not with a fix-it mentality but with the humble and courageous vocation to listen, to see, to engage, to act and to love.

Wisdom means living the counterintuitive, countercultural life of Jesus in the midst of all the lives, relationships and places God loves. Naming wisdom this way places it in real time and does so with life-altering implications. It means the church doesn't celebrate just the good news of eternal salvation but also the good news that the same God who died for the world's redemption also offers life-giving love on ordinary days in places of comfort and of desperation.

When Christians affirm that wisdom is who God is and how God acts, we affirm that it is what makes, explains and redeems the world. "For God so loved the world that he gave his only Son, so that everyone who believes in him may not perish but may have eternal life" is not merely a religious claim but a reality claim (John 3:16). Staking your trust on this affirmation means living wisely, living in ways that correspond with reality. If "God is love," to love is to embody reality. Talk of love may be true, but actually loving is wise; it's God's truth and character lived in your own context.

When Jesus names, touches and heals the leper, he enacts wisdom that doesn't look and walk away. But that may be more wisdom and more reality than we want. The "insights" in any claim to wisdom are only as valuable as their correspondence to reality. Brilliance can easily lack wisdom if it fails to grasp and live in reality. This is why Jesus says we must become like children. That's the wisdom of life in the kingdom of God.

In biblical terms, wisdom leads people to acts of courage in places of need. Wisdom moves into a neighborhood school and serves with humility. Wisdom does business with honesty and humility, even when it means losing clients. Wisdom pursues the rescue of victims of sex trafficking, even when it is slow, invisible and dangerous. Wisdom seeks the shalom of your city or town, especially with your enemies. Wisdom gives money away with joy. Wisdom confesses and lives out of weakness.

All this means that we can *see* wisdom, not just hear about it. It bears the names of people who demonstrate it:

- Aaron, who called his church to "foster the city" in response to the huge number of foster children needing homes in Washington, D.C.

- Janet, who daily loved, challenged and formed public high school students in the San Francisco Bay Area

- Tom, who took his abused life and learned to make short films that helped heal the lives of others

- Theogene, who faced the truth about political abuse and found the courage to admit and confront it, even at the risk of his own life

A Global Cry

We are in a crossroads period, a time of almost unparalleled personal and global turbulence. We are seeking to understand a way forward, but it's not simple. It isn't so much insight that people seek as it is a broad convergence right now of people everywhere crying, to whoever might be listening, "Fix it!" In this time of turmoil, people want action that makes things better.

War, economic upheaval, random violence, human trafficking, unemployment, terrorism, failed nations, emerging nations, disappointing rescues, cultural polarization, global warming, HIV/AIDS, pervasive fear—all these move from backdrop to forefront again and again. These ominous and recurrent sirens distress and discourage us. We want them to stop. We long not so much for ideas as for action that relieves and renews. We want someone to *do something* that actually changes things.

Many who long for a fix for our macro and micro issues know this: the fix must be real, it must be transformative, and it must fit the need. No fantasy or idealism will do. No shuffling of words without action. No generic, globalized response.

In biblical terms, this is a cry for wisdom. Of course, that isn't what most would say or recognize as their hunger. Even many in the church wouldn't put it that way, because we too think what we need is something more pragmatic and *realpolitik* than we expect wisdom to be.

Biblical wisdom, however, is not sage, religious advice that leaves action as an option for overachievers. It is character in action in the face of life's real needs. No action, no wisdom. God's wisdom is not a pathway of escape but a road of faithful engagement. Wisdom is not an insider tip for the spiritually privileged. God's wisdom breaks passivity and leads to action. If we don't take action, our house is built on sand, even if we profess that it's built on rock. This mix of understanding, action and context is what God has given us in Jesus Christ and asks us to follow. Instincts for action are justifiable and valid, theologically as well as socially, not least if we are people of the incarnation, cross and resurrection.

Of course, those outside the church who cry for solutions and change rarely recognize any relevance in what the good news offers. But the same is true for many inside the church. The prevalent separation between form and content, between words and actions, between voice and touch is rife both inside and outside the church. But biblical wisdom doesn't hide in private: "Wisdom cries out in the street; in the squares she raises her voice" (Proverbs 1:20).

WISDOM CALLS

Just as that imagery in Proverbs suggests, wisdom calls out to us and to a world in need. What she says gives life to us and to those around us. Whatever our work or ministry may be, whether we're in the marketplace or in the nonprofit world, whether we're artists or pastors, we all need to know what gives life and how to share that with others.

This means wisdom grounds our lives in communion with God, and it strengthens and shapes us to live wisely wherever we find ourselves. Wisdom calls out our identity and cheers our living response. Wisdom underscores that we are called to follow Jesus, who is wisdom incarnate, and to demonstrate wisdom by letting it become flesh in us. Finding wisdom is like the difference between finding a bottle of water and finding a rushing river. Both have their place, but only the latter is sufficient for a lifetime—and for far more than just us.

Jesus is the incarnation of wisdom—God's truth and character made flesh in the world. Following Jesus means stepping into the incarnational life in time and space. It means engaging in the ministry of the foolishness of the cross that is the wisdom of God (1 Corinthians 1:18). Wisdom is counterintuitive to a culture of self-interest bent on self-flourishing, often over and against the whole. Yet this is the evidence of the wisdom of God working its way into and out through our lives.

The lost way of wisdom is foundational to the way of Jesus. In it you will find your life, and you will flourish.

Practice

Make a list of people who seem to demonstrate biblical wisdom, those who live God's truth and character in context. They may be people you know personally or whom you have witnessed from afar.

- What is it about their actions that demonstrates wisdom?

- What evidence of human flourishing do you observe in or around them?

- If possible, consider interviewing one or more of these people to learn more about what motivates and encourages them. What do you learn that's surprising? Helpful? Discouraging?

9

THE WAY
OF SUFFERING

We who have known safety, health and full stomachs have little or no problem with thinking about the potential goodness of God's call. But when suffering comes into the picture, not least suffering that may come because we are following God's will and purpose, we are suddenly chilled. If we're made to flourish, how can suffering belong?

This is yet another Promised Land assumption. In that paradigm, the whole point of following God's way is to get away from what is undesirable, to separate ourselves from experiences of pain, to leave suffering behind and to live in the land of milk and honey. If it turns out that suffering is involved, the Promised Land seems to be a fraud.

Well, what if suffering is actually a sign of being in exile instead? What if our call is really one of deeply entering and loving a world full of suffering? What if we understand calling and vocation to be living out God's life of love for just such a world? We still may not like the implications, but they are consistent with both the world we know and the God we serve.

Remembering Where We Are

At the risk of repetition, it's vital that we remember where we live and how that affects our expectations regarding God's call.

If we live in middle- or upper-middle-class America and are part of the dominant culture and have reasonable resources and freedoms (even if it's not everything we could dream of having), we're part of a small percentage of the world. The norm for most people in our world includes neither adequate resources nor the freedoms we experience every day. Their days are about trying to find enough of almost anything: food, clean water, safe housing, basic education, freedom from violent predators, medical care.

Spending time in such circumstances—just visiting, let alone living there—would be suffering for most reading these pages. Yet it's normative for billions today. If our vocation—hearing and living in response to the love of God for the sake of the world—is our calling, we need to grasp that it includes following Jesus into the lives and places of such suffering. To do this will mean in some way "the sharing of his sufferings" (Philippians 3:10).

Seeking a call that evades suffering is a decision neither to follow Jesus nor to live in the real world. How can we read the Gospels and hear Jesus say, "Take up [your] cross and follow me" (Matthew 16:24), and believe that isn't for us? Suffering is not the goal of following Jesus. It will, however, be a consequence, because it's a call to love the real and suffering world. The "cross" we take up isn't an accident of circumstances but a willful choice to imitate the love of Jesus, who took up his cross out of love and calls us to do likewise.

From a kingdom perspective, vocation isn't primarily about how to find fulfillment and satisfaction. The frequent assumption is that we seek to find the perfect way to get the most out of life as the unique and wonderful people we are. That's more a reflection of narcissism than healthy self-esteem, let alone Christlike humility and servanthood. There will be joy in our call, but that is different from making the pursuit of happiness our priority.

Jesus doesn't call us to make us martyrs. He calls us to make us like himself. This requires a process of transformation. Our attention can and does gradually shift from ourselves and our struggles to the people and needs we're trying to serve in the light of God's great mercy and love.

Zac is as close as a brother to me. For fifteen years, we've shared life from different parts of the world. He's in Uganda, and I'm in the United States. He comes from a very simple Ugandan home; he didn't experience electricity until he was twelve. But he eventually got a PhD in theology at the University of Edinburgh. He has been a leader in the church of Uganda, and he has vigorously entered into ministry in many other African settings as well. Until recently, he had been serving as a bishop in Kampala.

One of my earliest memories of Zac was in a meeting with many Westerners about the need for more theological depth and education for Christian leaders in the Majority World. Zac agreed, but then he went on to say, "But there are some things the church in the Majority World can teach those in the West."

"Like what?" someone asked.

"Like having joy in the midst of suffering."

Today Zac is putting his life on the line every day in Uganda as he stands against government injustices that cause much pain and suffering in his country, especially among children. His life is at risk. He is a threat to the regime. He is a truth teller. The suffering Zac and his family face because of their willingness to tell the truth and to stand against the abuse of power is real. But to Zac, the suffering isn't his; it is that of those he represents and speaks for daily. He could easily avoid it. He could step away and see it as too big, as not his problem, as beyond his ability to solve and as pointless. Instead, he has taken up his cross.

The vast percentage of people who suffer in the world today do so because of circumstances they didn't choose and can't control. Children. Women. God's people themselves are among these. The "we" who suffer daily include hundreds of millions of brothers and sisters in the faith as well as the wider circle of other human beings made in the image of God.

In the name of Jesus Christ, we have the privilege of choosing to move toward those who suffer. This is part of maturing in the call to live as God's people in the world. We want to be an expression of the heart and love of God, to act with compassion and justice. This is love that encounters other people who are just like us: people with relationships, with needs, with hopes.

These risk takers are people like Zac from Kampala, Prodip from Dacca, Beth from Minneapolis, Joshua from Redding and Sunni from Los Angeles. Each of their stories has become real to me. Each of them has taken the risk to be known, to tell the truth, to live into the raw challenges before them, to try to show up in the name of Christ out of their sense of calling.

It may be that particular needs rise out of our own backgrounds or circumstances, and we are called to engage there in a specialized or sustained way. It may be as a result of where we live or the geographic or ethnic heritage we have. But the point is that we carry out our general vocation by identifying with the suffering of others in the name of Jesus Christ.

So many people I know today have chosen, quietly and genuinely, to do this. Some have moved across the world. Some have moved into a different neighborhood in their own city or town. Some have become foster or adoptive parents. Some volunteer in schools where children are dramatically underserved. Some have given up their status and money to do work that they consider their spiritual vocation. Some live daily with the threat of their own demise as they stand in the face of injustice. The price is a form of suffering that they carry daily.

Andy's father refused to talk with him when he gave up law school to serve the inner-city kids he had come to love. James makes food for gang members in Los Angeles every day and has been mugged several times afterward. Mary is a banker who risked her career and reputation to expose internal injustices in loan policies. Pete carried the burden of leading a church in truth telling and confession after serial sexual abuse by a former youth pastor, and his life has been marked by this tragic offense. None of these people went looking for these challenges, but they followed Jesus and the challenges found them.

All of these are examples of people who chose to include in their lives the suffering of others. They chose to live a call to love like Jesus.

Suffering Because of the Call

Sometimes people suffer not because the world is suffering but because doing some things is so hard it causes suffering. Here I'm thinking of an array of efforts made by people who suffer because of their work. Artists are at the top of this list. "Suffering artist" is one of the catchphrases that captures how pervasive this is, and for good reason. The thought may come to mind of an artist suffering as his income affords him only a bad apartment and cheap food. But for someone who is an artist—whatever his apartment and food—the work he finds himself doing often involves suffering.

Some of this has to do with pursuing creative expression that seems essential and urgent to the artist yet seems neither to those around her. This creates its own dissonance and pain. Most serious artists try to express in their art some aspects or dimensions of being human that they find no other language for. Their art itself is therefore both primal and illusive. Artists often feel that they're going to erupt with something in the core of their life, and yet it isn't readily or easily released. The struggle feels imperative to the artist—as basic as life itself—but the marginalization artists feel from the community around them intensifies the feelings. Many Christian artists especially feel this isolation and wonder whether it's not only isolation from the church but also from God.

All of this contributes to suffering that comes from trying to be an expresser of a feeling, conviction or perspective. The creative act is frequently complex, subtle, indirect, uncertain, slow, necessary, compelling. To be an artist who seeks to do seminal creative work within limits that normally exist and that explore some of the most profound human experiences or feelings is very difficult.

Throughout history, the artist—sacred or otherwise—has felt at the margins of community. This adds to a deep sense of carrying a burden, which is often for the very community that doesn't see or recognize or understand that the artist gives her whole being to what she creates. Yes, "suffering artist" is only partly about the apartment and the food.

Others who suffer in their vocations do so because they're pursuing change that is painfully slow or has a severe cost, emotionally or otherwise. Social reformers—Martin Luther King Jr., Nelson Mandela and Aung San Suu Kyi, for example—pay a severe price to do something that is very difficult to accomplish. It requires their life.

The same may be said in different terms of people who give themselves to an effort that requires saying no to many other parts of life for the sake of their commitment. Caring for a child with special needs, perhaps providing decades of acute care, or taking care of a parent in declining health might absorb all that someone has to give. Or, quite differently, perhaps someone suffers in the isolation of sustained research and the acute loneliness that comes with it. Or someone lives with a physical or emotional disability, an impairment from birth, or an injury from domestic violence or war. Suffering is a pervasive part of trying to live in such situations—let alone live honestly and faithfully and live both in and beyond the difficulty.

I've written before about my friend Dustin, who is one of the most inspiring people in my life. Born with severe cerebral palsy, Dustin can't walk or speak, but he shines. In honesty and struggle, in faith and love, he carries the vocation he can have in this time while acknowledging a vocation he'll have only in eternity. He knows he lives in exile. He knows he's made to flourish. He says this in a poetic, brief essay, "*My*

Most Important Decision," which he wrote when he was a teenager. It's his testimony of a called life.

It really is like letting very doomed emotions peel like a banana.

Issues in my silent mind are causing domineering tiles of negative thoughts to foolishly build.

They tempt me to stop working on my noticed strength and not write.

Teased by cerebral palsy, it is tempting to give up.

Titled notion, about imagined told would have been emerges as self-pity.

If doing time on self-pity roller coaster got any etymology awards my canceled voice would win.

Great fool that I am, I get used dissected genuine brain tissue.

Tests my ability to laugh.

Emerging in the usual spot in my mind is normality.

It is nine sane daring thoughts in a dappled dish.

At manly morning of Good Friday someone heard my worried lost story.

He daringly leant me his non-solicited attitude.

Barely the action of a tall king, he bailed the world out.

Titled Jesus adjusted man's luck.

Borrowed temptation for self-pity ails my soul.

Deciding to trust Jesus turns this around. The after tiled wall tumbles.

Bright ideas enter my mind. Bit by the love of Jesus, I let nets of sorrowful attitudes escape.

I am a writer.

God has given me this ability.

I need to remember Easter.

Eternity is my time to run. Now is my time to write.

Dustin knows and lives his call. He flourishes in exile. He waits.

Practice

Work on cultivating a language of lament by collecting a few psalms, poems, hymns, popular songs, works of art or other expressions that particularly resonate with you.

- Find ways to incorporate these into your regular prayer, worship or other devotional times—whether you're crying out on your own behalf, for loved ones or for others around the world.

- When you read, watch or listen to the news, make note of particular needs locally and globally for which you can offer intercessory prayers of lament.

10

SO, WHAT DOES GOD CALL *ME* TO DO?

You may have presumed that the personal and distinctive issue of call was going to be the subject of every chapter in this book. I hope it's clear why we are only now able to come to the question "What does God call me to do?" Call is primarily about who we are and what we do all the time. Call isn't measured by outcomes—how much we achieve or accomplish—but through the process of following Jesus in and through it all. In the end, call is about continuous formation into the likeness of Jesus Christ far more than it is about finding direction or getting a job. "Strive first for the kingdom of God and his righteousness, and all these things will be given to you as well" (Matthew 6:33).

The Bible includes some dramatic moments in the Old and New Testaments that involve God giving individuals a clear and personal call to a very distinctive mission: Adam and Eve, Abraham, Moses, David, Mary, Joseph, Paul and so many more. The question is what to make of these examples. The revelation of God's character in action must be lived out by God's people in light of God's purposes to bless them and pass blessings through them to the nations. This is the big arc, the calling God gave to Israel and that continues through the birth of the church at Pentecost and beyond. As members of the whole community of God, our primary call is to respond through discipleship to Jesus, by the power of the Holy Spirit.

CALL AND FORMATION

Our experience of God's call comes in whatever way God chooses. Some have defined moments of experiencing God's call that are similar to conversion. For many others, call emerges over time through a series of experiences or relationships that guide them in various directions.

The process of formation is multifaceted since we are multidimensional people. Our spiritual life has many strands, which Jesus seems to suggest by quoting the first commandment: we love God with all our heart, mind, soul and strength (Matthew 22:37). Our lives have many parts, all of which find their deepest resolution and satisfaction in offerings of love to God. God takes who we are and makes us into who God wants us to be.

However, that isn't easily or consistently done. All kinds of things happen that can challenge or confuse us about call. For example, we may feel called to work in a particular place, but as that unfolds, we encounter enormous difficulties or even opposition. We are confronted by inner turmoil, circumstances or people that make living God's call much harder than we had anticipated. This experience isn't at all uncommon, and it's a formational one.

I've certainly been in circumstances when doing what I believed I was called to do was painful and difficult. One of the most challenging was a time when I felt I was the wrong pastor for the church I was serving. This was many years ago, and to this day I'm not sure whether it was God's call that I serve there. What I am confident of is that God used the challenges and difficulties of that season to form me into a different person; the Lord refined and remade me at a deep level during those days. Everything about my own call since that time has been enhanced in both quality and character. Though I'm not sure it was God's call that I pastor that church, it was surely God's call that I was changed as I worked there. I went seeking to be an agent of formation; I left being transformed.

Central to God's call is the ongoing work of our own spiritual formation—that we may become "mature in Christ" (Colossians 1:28). Jesus' disciples desperately need depth. Superficial Christians living superficial lives are not the witness Jesus intends. We are to grow in depth, like trees with roots deep in the soil of the world and watered by God's Word, in season and out (Psalm 1).

CALL AND THE GUIDANCE OF THE SPIRIT

As should be plain by now, a call in the most profound and pervasive sense doesn't require special illumination by the Holy Spirit. The primary call on our lives is to follow Jesus in all we do—this isn't a secret God hides and has to be coaxed into divulging.

The gift of the Holy Spirit in followers' lives contributes to an expectation that God now universally and necessarily personalizes our call. Life becomes a puzzle, and the Holy Spirit is the puzzle master who provides the clues and then the answers to all of them. In this approach, our vocation is to pursue God's direction on a step-by-step basis through special revelation. But is this what Scripture indicates to be God's intention?

It can easily be inferred that the dramatic moments of call in the lives of some biblical characters should be normative for all of the people of God. Furthermore, it seems reasonable to expect God's guidance or call in relation to all levels of concern—an inference built out of various biblical invitations, such as James's comment that "you do not have, because you do not ask" (James 4:2) and Paul's urging that the church "let your requests be made known to God" (Philippians 4:6). If we earnestly ask what God wants us in particular to do, then, the logic goes, we should reasonably expect God to guide us.

However, let's think carefully about what's happening in this process of interpretation. First John 4:1 instructs us to "test the spirits" so we are guided by the truth and by the Spirit, not by simply using Christian language to baptize desire. I remember an especially beautiful female missionary who returned to the United States and told me that, the week before she returned, she'd received five different proposals of marriage, each claiming the Holy Spirit had led them to propose. It wasn't hard to understand why these five men wanted the Holy Spirit to lead them in this way, but clearly that wasn't God's call.

This illustrates why there must always be humility and caution in claiming to be led by the Holy Spirit. We have to be sure that the inferences we draw from our understanding of the Holy Spirit—who is, after all, the Spirit of God the Father and God the Son—are about the same things as the Father and the Son. Therefore, the major revelation of God in

Scripture concerns the passions of God for the re-creation of all things after the likeness of Jesus Christ. Special guidance is and can be given, but it can also be an avenue for spiritual make-believe, and we need to mature in faith and wisdom so we can more likely tell the difference.

The process of understanding the Spirit's guidance is best done in community. It isn't a private act of discernment but one that emerges as we live in relation to brothers and sisters who help lead us to listen to our own hearts and to listen for God's. To do so wisely and not self-servingly or distortedly, we need friends in Christ who share in this process of listening and trusting. Together we are the dwelling place of the Spirit.

CALL AND THE FRUIT OF THE SPIRIT

The evidence that we're hearing and living the call of God is the fruit of the Holy Spirit in our lives: "love, joy, peace, patience, kindness, generosity, faithfulness, gentleness, and self-control" (Galatians 5:22-23). These fruit are the outgrowth of seeking and living God's call. They are the tangible evidence of God's presence that produces in and through us qualities that point to the source of our life, the gracious activity and mercy of God toward us.

If the call of our life is that we become like Jesus Christ—that our lives begin to mirror the character and compassion, righteousness and justice of God—the fruit of the Spirit is a vital sign of that trajectory. It isn't too much to suggest that, just as biological fruit has its seasons of flourishing and of waiting to develop, the fruit of the Spirit has seasons.

I remember, for example, dreaming about things I'd one day be doing—being married, serving as a pastor, getting to do more writing. These all happened eventually, but later than I would have wanted or imagined at an earlier stage. In retrospect, I'm glad for the timing and think much better things happened than if I had tried to force the fruit to maturity rather than trust God's deeper, hidden work and timing.

In the meantime, there is waiting and uncertainty. There can be blight and disease. Fruit growing is no simple business organically, nor is it spiritually. Growing fruit that looks like Jesus is a process that takes time, seems slow and can be uncertain. Its full maturity internally takes longer than its external appearance may suggest. All of that is just fine, because that is what fruit requires.

When our lives begin to reflect love, joy, peace and other fruit, it's a powerful witness to the comprehensive purposes of God. As we mature in Christ, we become ever more alike in our character (which is to be like that of Jesus himself) and ever more distinct in living our lives (which is to manifest God's creativity and gifts to each of us). To put it simply, we're called to Christ, called to become like Christ and called to express our lives in Christ.

CALL AND SCRIPTURE

As we mature in the faith, the Bible is a very important element in our growing knowledge of God and of God's purposes in the world. Scripture unlocks God's hopes for us and for our call. The Bible—as we read the whole in light of the parts and the parts in light of the whole—needs to form us and our theological and spiritual imaginations. Nothing else is as critical as this. We need to learn to read Scripture well, with careful thought and reflection—not using it as a spiritual version of a Ouija board, Rorschach test or dart board but as a profound narrative and guide to form and inform our faith and our call.

Examples of abusing Scripture for the sake of guidance are legendary. In fact, we might do it even when we're trying not to. Reading the Bible well includes, for example, not letting the narrative incidents become random metaphors for our lives and circumstances. Not all difficult times are necessarily wildernesses, not all challenges are the River Jordan, not every threat is a giant in the land. Learning the Scriptures well and letting them form our confidence in the character and passions of God help us hear God's call.

We live our narrative from the biblical narrative. Our story of call is of a piece with the long, varied stories of God's call to people throughout the Bible, and it is amid the communion of saints past and present who have been caught up in the great drama of God's faithfulness and love. *Our* call is both the same—common because God is the shared source—and unique—distinct because we're different. The rootedness of our life in the faithfulness of God made known in Scripture interacts with our experience and grounds our call in the Living Word.

CALL AND COMMUNITY

We do our best discernment with other followers of Jesus. In an honest community of love, where we know and see one another in truth and hope, we can be a great help in reflecting back to others who they are, what gifts they seem to have and how we see God using them in the church or in the wider community. This can really help clarify our self-understanding and recast our communion with God and one another. If we think God is guiding us, but no one in the body of Christ that best knows us can stand alongside us and affirm it, that sense of guidance is likely doubtful and may be worth reconsidering before acting. The opposite is also the case: some in the body may affirm us, but we would do well to look for corroboration beyond that close circle.

Community comes in many forms, but we all need it to hear and also to live our call. We follow Jesus together. I've been part of a pastor's covenant group for thirty years. It's a group of diverse men and women, and we've shared life in all the seasons you can imagine—some of the most painful and some of the most joyful, and everything in between. Listening and loving together over decades has changed all of us and given us the gift of seeing and understanding call in times of clarity and of confusion. It's like being on a road trip together for decades.

CALL AND THE GIFTS OF THE SPIRIT

The gifts of God are manifestations of the Spirit for the sake of ministry in the church and the world. The New Testament affirms that each person in the body of Christ has gifts given for the sake of the wider church community.

We could anticipate that our sense of call will afford us the chance to put our own spiritual gifts to good use often. But God isn't required to use our gifts in a constant or predictable way. They may be variously used, and they may be needed in varied settings over the course of life. We usually find the greatest satisfaction when we have the opportunity to use our gifts. Doing so is not our right, nor is it a violation if we can't do so, but our gifts often give us significant clues to how we might serve the body of Christ.

Discernment of our gifts is a work of the Holy Spirit, of the beloved community and of our own availability. We have to put ourselves in places of service to Christ's body to see what we might contribute. Some of this involves gifts for building up various aspects of the institutional life of the church: evangelists, pastors, preachers, teachers, encouragers, administrators, worship leaders, elders, deacons. These gifts can be applied across generations and in all kinds of forms in which the body might gather—house churches, congregations of all sizes and types, parachurch ministries and so on.

CALL AND PERSONAL STRENGTHS

In addition to spiritual gifts for the building up the body of Christ, we have personal strengths and traits that can be very important in living out our call. Again, since not everyone has choices or opportunities, it's generally a great gift when our strengths and traits can be discovered, developed and put to good use. The more this happens, the better it is for everyone involved.

I have some strengths and abilities, but I'm very aware that I also have all kinds of limits. Temperament, personality, habits and background all contribute to my awareness of myself. They also affect the things that interest me and engage my imagination, tap into my energies and allow me to do what

I can to contribute in the workplace or elsewhere. Living into my sense of call has required time and help from others in understanding my abilities and dealing with my limitations, fears and diversions. It has taken a community to surround and encourage me to develop and to try out what I have talent to do and what I can do despite not having much talent in it.

We all have to come to terms with our strengths and other personal traits that contribute to our sense of call. I might imagine a call to be a gifted violinist, but nothing in my life would make it seem like the direction I should go. That's very different from needing training or encouragement to do what I might be able to accomplish. We have to do some honest sorting in light of who we are and what we believe is relevant to our life and talent. In this effort comes freedom to live our own life and not to try to live someone else's.

CALL AND CONTEXT

Bruce leads an urban ministry in a very poor inner-city community in New Jersey. In some ways, he lives and serves at a sociological crossroads of call. The ministry is organized and led by a board of professional people who are seeking to engage in serving such a needy community. They do this as volunteers out of their own sense of call. They include a dentist who gives away his dentistry to improve kids' lives.

Then there are the teenagers involved in the ministry, who are seeking a better life, one that they may or may not understand to be God's call. In most cases, their choices involve dramatically different options than those of the dentist. Still, God has a call on their lives too.

All of us may be in exile, but we live in different parts of it. The part we're in affects what we think we may hear as God's call. Every setting has opportunities and challenges that affect our call. If you're a parent and one of your children develops a serious illness that demands sustained attention and care, your call is to do whatever you can to provide for his or her needs. You may still have a job to go to or other responsibilities, but caring for your child is your calling, and there is no need to "discern" it.

But a need doesn't necessitate a call, as many have said. A setting doesn't necessarily require that we embrace all its concerns or its circumstances. But, in most cases, we need to engage at both the local and the global level. And we need to ask, what are the realities of this local place before us in our immediate context, and what are the global realities beyond us that are part of the wider context? For most people reading this book, our calling needs to be glocal—global and local— each aspect informing and shaping the other. "Think globally, act locally" is one way this can be played out.

We care about global poverty and the ways it affects our response to immigrants locally. We hear about a remote war and meet refugees who come to our town. We know that education is a global concern, and we commit ourselves to do something at the local schools to make a difference. We hear about the global need for mature disciples, and we make it a priority to understand discipleship beyond just our ethnicity or class, so we ask people of other backgrounds to teach us. To do otherwise in today's world seems to be shortsighted. This is even truer for the people who seek to follow the One who is Lord of all.

Call and Conviction

Call usually arises out of our most passionate conviction. We give ourselves with deep commitment and love, joy and sacrifice to the focus of our passion. Our faith in Jesus Christ combines with our experience in the world to raise up an awareness and concern for certain things more than other things. As this occurs, we begin to see the world in particular ways that further stimulate our thoughts and feelings, education and actions. We start acting out of a set of growing convictions that we should pay attention to someone or something that seems necessary or important.

If we're serious about following Jesus, our question needs

to be, "What are the things about which Jesus would call me to have the greatest passion?" It's important to read and internalize the Gospels so we become people who see and care about the world in ways that are more than just a reflection of our own culture, background or bias. When we begin to ask what God's concerns are and how we can enter into sharing those concerns in community with others, our calling moves from just a personal concern to a shared conviction with others whose convictions also lead their sense of calling.

I got to see this all the time when I served as a pastor of a diverse congregation of people who had all kinds of concerns for themselves and the world around us. I think of how I've seen the convictions of one become the convictions of a few, which becomes motivation for the majority of the church to begin to act in relationship to local and global needs. In one case, it was a very needy local junior high. In another, it was the national crisis of mass incarceration of African American men. For another, it was the urgency of personal evangelism. For another, it was intercession for those needing healing. The call to respond to these important needs rose as they sought to share "the mind of Christ" and to let it show in tangible form in the world. They couldn't do everything, but they began to know they could do something and let the heart of their convictions lead them to do so.

CALL AND TIME

We receive all our time as a gift, and we can offer virtually all our activities as a context for living out our vocation as Christ's disciples. These include personal hygiene, dressing, finding water and food, preparing a meal, eating, moving around in the physical world, talking, listening, doing work, attempting to secure safety and more. In these activities we demonstrate our stewardship of the natural world, our care for our bodies and possibly for the bodies and lives of others, our relationships, the risks we face and the priorities that use our time. All these are the baseline of our daily lives, so doing these ordinary things is part of our existence and also part of our vocation as disciples.

In light of this, all our time is for the sake of our vocation. But most reading this book are probably asking, "How should we use our primary time for our primary calling?" This brings us to the question of work.

CALL AND WORK

It should be abundantly clear by now that all God's people are called. The language of call belongs not only to those in formal roles of Christian leadership but to all of God's people. Though the Protestant Reformation in the sixteenth century affirmed the ministry of the whole people of God, most groups within Protestantism simply swapped the clericalism of priests for the clericalism of pastors. Martin Luther saw things more holistically:

> All our work in the field, in the garden, in the city, in the home, in struggle, in government—to what does it all amount before God except child's play, by means of which God is pleased to give his gifts in the field, at home, and everywhere? These are the masks of our Lord God, behind which he wants to be hidden and to do all things.[1]

The sacred/secular divide has continued despite a theology to the contrary. As a consequence, "call" is still the domain of the "sacred" role of the public Christian leader and not the language used for those whose energies are spent in "secular" forms of work. This is a travesty, since it suggests that 98 percent of the Christian world is "just working" rather than seeing what they are doing as an enactment of God's call. This is additionally galling when the work of the 98 percent is demeaned as "secular," though they're providing the financial means for the church's ministry to occur.

In the broadest sense of call, people can and should be affirmed to live God's call as faithful disciples in whatever work setting they may find themselves. This is an enactment of their human identity and value, of their call to love God with all they are and to love their neighbors (bosses, colleagues, clients and so on) as themselves. It means seeking to enact God's love and justice toward any we touch or know about through our work and its impact.

This may mean watching for people who need attention or encouragement. It may mean thinking creatively about how to make the workplace more human and more fruitful. It may mean being willing to speak up about workplace injustices or about inequities that might affect morale and performance, especially for those on the lower end of the pay scale.

More specifically, those of us who can make choices about the types of work we do (true of most reading this but not true of most people in the world) can ask God to guide us in the best use of our skills and abilities in relation to work. Here's where all the distinctions of personality, temperament, ability and circumstances say a great deal to us about what we do with our work life. Making wise choices about this means we can make as strong a contribution as possible to the stewardship of the earth, the workplace and the society at large.

CALL AND MONDAY MORNING

We are called to work. Our whole lives, including our daily

labor, are part of our call to be followers of Jesus. If our daily labor is to make furniture, to sell insurance, to create art, to do wealth management, to be a musician, to be a teacher or to wash dishes, we are to live it as an offering to God.

At the very least, our job is a setting for our call to live and work as a disciple. We go to work called to speak and act as someone who follows Jesus. The integrity of our work, the honesty and diligence of our labor, the commitment to fairness and justice, the intention to serve with humility and competence—these are all outgrowths of embracing the responsibility of our workplace as a Christian.

It's often the case that the work itself is our calling. The elements of the tasks or the purposes of the work capture what we feel called to contribute to the world, to our country, to our town or to our neighborhood. If you're a manager, for example, you can certainly feel a call to foster a healthy, thriving, fruitful workplace. That may be your calling within the wider purposes of a company or enterprise. Artists who make paintings or make music can find in that labor the convergence of their creativity and their need to express their talents, and hopefully earn an income in doing so. Financial advisers can carry out that work in the confidence that they're adding to the resources that help individuals or institutions survive and even thrive.

Everyone's work is a setting for their call as a disciple, but not everyone's work may be their calling. Lots of people work simply to do what they can to make money to sustain themselves and others. This is a good thing. Doing work is a healthy part of our human experience. It's a good use of our time and of our physical and emotional health. It's part of our stewardship of the earth, of our mind, of our bodies.

This doesn't mean all work is intrinsically satisfying or meaningful or equal to any other. Some work is illegal or immoral. Some work is drudgery and abusive in its repetition or mindlessness. Some work may be necessary for economic survival, but we may feel like it's a distraction from our primary call. Just ask a starving artist how he feels about being a waiter on the side.

But what matters most is the need for faithful disciples in virtually all spheres of work to make the contributions they can by exercising their strengths. This is actually quite a lot to accomplish. Being able to do so with character and to earn money that can help themselves, their family and others have the resources necessary for life is a wonderful gift.

Call motivates, empowers, dignifies and inspires our work. "Whatever you do, in word or deed, do everything in the name of the Lord Jesus, giving thanks to God the Father through him" (Colossians 3:17).

CALL AND MONEY

As has been frequently observed, Jesus says more about money than any other topic. His warnings are many about the ways money can distort our sense of power and influence, our relationships with others, our dependency on God, our freedom to follow in the way of Jesus. In other words, money can affect our call.

We need to admit that money, our fear of it, our misgivings about it and our attraction to it are factors in how we hear and follow God's call. No one approach to money is the definitive Christian approach, but it would be naive to ignore the influence money has on people's sense of call.

That we must make money in order to live is too often an unspoken aspect of our sense of call. A fair wage is a minimal expectation. Freedom from worry over basic necessities is a legitimate hope, and though it's not globally common to reach this level, many in the United States and elsewhere do.

Some feel their call is to make far more than they need to sustain themselves and their family, especially in the Western world. The first issue of call in such cases is whether the money is justly earned and used in a morally responsible way. Assuming it is, what is the call on the person's life in relation to all those additional resources?

Since most reading this book live in a capitalist society, it's worth pausing to recognize how much is done in the world as an expression of God's call through the money and wealth that capitalism creates. For example, virtually every church and Christian nonprofit, pastor and missionary is funded because of gifts from people who make money and give it away as a part of their Christian vocation.

This is not a rationale, nor a rationalization, for capitalism. As long as it's the system we have and as long as we remain within it but free to critique its abuses, Christians also need to acknowledge that mammon is critical for kingdom work. Those who provide it do a very important and necessary task. Sadly and unfairly, many businesspeople who make money as part of their calling are treated as second-rank members of the church's ministry, even though that ministry couldn't happen without their talent and generosity. If it weren't for wealth creation, Christian churches, institutions and organizations all over the world would not be able to carry out their call to share the love of Jesus Christ in the ways they do.

Money and call are frequently intertwined, and maturing disciples need to be honest and clear about how that affects them and how to remain free to hear and follow the call of God. We need honest brothers and sisters to help us discern this, and we need far greater candor in the body of Christ about the possibilities and pitfalls of money in relation to our call.

CALL AND VOLUNTEERISM

Beyond the call to family, community and work, many have at least some time for volunteer effort as a further expression of call. Such work may emerge out of convictions about needs near or far that make claims on our concerns and priorities.

Let's imagine a person whose primary work every day takes a large amount of time and is done out of a desire to do that work as an offering to God. But beyond this, maybe in relation to quite different needs, a person may have a concern for violence in her community, for race relations, for the homeless population, for a needy neighborhood school, for sex trafficking in South Asia. Volunteering time, talent, money, support, thought, energy and passion in trying to make a difference is an expression of vocation.

For example, we might think of a person who organizes a fund drive because it will help, not because he is good at fund drives. Or we think of a retired architect who volunteers with joy to love very young children in a needy school. This isn't a match with her life work, but it's undoubtedly a match with her sense of call.

Does every disciple need to volunteer for a church program? No. It's not possible, since there often aren't enough jobs. But every disciple does have a role in helping build up the body of Christ.

Does every disciple need to volunteer for the wider scene? Yes. It's always needed and possible. Every disciple needs to help care for the world around us in Jesus' name.

The Process Is the Goal

The very process of spiritual formation is itself God's call on us. Seeking God's transformation in our lives is both the process and the end. Following Jesus is not a destination; we do not arrive. We wake and live and sleep and wake again to follow another day. This is the extraordinary spiritual road trip that disciples have always known and that all disciples must discover anew.

Practice

On individual index cards, brainstorm some thoughts about what you're discerning in your own life about the various aspects of call listed below. Review your cards to see what patterns emerge. Are there connections you may not have noticed before? Which areas might benefit from more focused discernment?

- *The guidance of the Spirit.* What is your experience of the Holy Spirit's guidance in your life? Do you tend to overemphasize or underemphasize spiritual illumination? How might you enlist your community to help "test the spirits" (1 John 4:1)?

- *Fruit of the Spirit (Galatians 5:22-23).* Which fruit are more evident in your life? Which less so? Which have you been working to cultivate?

- *Scripture.* What Scripture texts have been particularly encouraging, challenging, comforting or rebuking for you? Are there particular biblical narratives you return to often or that especially resonate with you?

- *Community.* Who are the friends, family, colleagues and peers you trust to help you in discernment and formation?

- *Gifts of the Spirit.* What do you believe to be your spiritual gifts? Are you able to use your gifts now? If so, in what ways? If not, how might you grieve or lament this?

- *Personal strengths.* What strengths and abilities are you able to use regularly? What would you like to use, though you haven't yet had the opportunity? Are there strengths you wish you had that are perhaps not realistic for you? Are there strengths others presume you have that don't feel true to who you are?

- *Context.* How has your culture, ethnicity, sociology, city, workplace or neighborhood shaped who you are and what you have to offer?

- *Convictions.* What are you passionate about?

- *Time.* How do you spend your time? What feels like "primary time"? Are there aspects of this you would like to change?

- *Work.* Which aspects of your work reflect your sense of call? Which less so? How can you fulfill your call to be "light and salt" at work, even if the work itself doesn't feel like a call?

- *Money.* How does your financial situation affect your sense of call?

- *Volunteering.* What are ways in which you can volunteer to help care for the world in Jesus' name?

FIRST THINGS—
SALT AND LIGHT

Each and all of God's people are called to live as followers of Jesus and to let it show in who we are and in what we do. The "called" are not a special subset who have certain tasks and functions in certain settings. The called are all of God's people living and serving throughout the world, in every country and town, in every neighborhood and home, wherever we can be found.

It is our voice and touch, in mutuality and in individuality, lived and offered, that can make God's presence tangible to others. We are God's plan. As the body of Christ, by the power of the Holy Spirit, we are to be the primary display of God's character and of God's purposes in the world. God uses all the means God chooses, but God's people are those upon whom God vests the most.

To step into the called life is to reverse the crisis of following Jesus today. It means regaining our footing about where we live, how we live and to what end we live. Getting these first things first in our hearts, minds, words and hands reframes everything else. It allows the simple clarity of realizing on any given day that the core of our life is about following Jesus. We don't follow the church. We don't follow our sociology. We wake up to follow Jesus Christ and let that relationship lead us to understand and engage in all the other steps we take.

Stepping into our calling means living in a fresh daily encounter of God's love in Jesus Christ. Following requires staying in close touch. It means keeping our sights clear when so much can distract us. But it also means living into the adventure of abundant life that Jesus longs for all of us to have. C. S. Lewis captured this well in his sermon "The Weight of Glory" when he said,

> Our Lord finds our desires not too strong but too weak. We are half-hearted creatures fooling about with drink and sex and ambition when infinite joy is offered us, like an ignorant child who wants to go on making mud pies in a slum because he can't imagine what is meant by the offer of a holiday at the sea. We are far too easily pleased.[1]

The crisis of following Jesus is that God's people fool about with far lesser ambition and settle in the slum when we are offered a holiday at the sea. That holiday is God's flourishing life—for us and for the world.

The call of following Jesus is to lead all humanity into that flourishing life. May we be people who know something of that journey as we get on the road together and give ourselves to the very life for which we are made and called.

First Things

What if Jesus' followers throughout the world—roughly two billion of us—were to seek each day simply to live our primary vocation: to love God and to love our neighbor? Or what if, for now, at least you and I did this?

For a vast percentage of us around the world, few choices of work are possible or relevant. Part of the injustice many suffer, of course, is a lack of different or more desirable choices. But all disciples, whatever our context, can seek to live our primary calling. Should we do this, our lives and our world would be significantly changed.

Bob was a finish carpenter who lived to make things. It was his craft, his art, his joy. What it didn't have was any particular connection to the God he worshiped, or so he thought. He made his money to do carpentry by working at a bank as a midlevel executive. He did his job at the office to pay for what he did later in his workshop. Carpentry was, as Bob said, "his" time. No family responsibilities, no work, no pressure, just artistry.

I remember the day he told me he had just begun to ask God what his artistry had to do with being a disciple. That was the start of a new day. It eventually led him to taking on two teenage boys as assistants in order to pass on to them what he knew and loved. He taught them everything he could about wood, design, technique—but even more about beauty and the God who made it. The art, he later said, was even more beautiful now because it had moved from being a privilege he hoarded to a gift he shared.

Sharon's parents taught her that the two most important things in life were her faith and her grades. The order of the two seemed to vary in practice, if not in declaration. As a family, they went to church weekly, if not more. But in college, Sharon was on her own, and getting the highest grades was her controlling compass. Her dorm was near Telegraph Avenue in Berkeley, and to and from class she was panhandled by homeless teenagers. One day she was mugged, and her backpack with her computer was stolen. Though most of what she had was replaced and her files recovered, she grew daily in hatred toward the teenagers asking for spare change, fearing for her safety and perhaps even more for the potential loss of her academic work. What she hated about them most, she said, was that they threatened her GPA, so it felt like they were taking her life.

As we talked, Sharon said she gave God the glory for her perfect GPA and saw it as a way to honor God, but she seemed blind to her own need to find significance and meaning through academic excellence. By the time she graduated, Sharon's heart and world had cracked open with the love of Jesus. This wasn't because she thought she was going to work with street kids but because she realized she couldn't say she loved God but continue to hate her enemy. The primary call of Jesus was redefining the rest of her life.

It would be hard for me to think of someone more competitive than Alan. Every corpuscle of his being was about winning. But after a significant emotional breakdown, he had given up. It was like all the air had gone out. He was beyond mellow; he was resigned, withdrawn. Alan was like a tiger asleep in a cage, and for several years I wasn't sure he would awaken.

The depression gradually lifted. The light of God's love that had seemed so illusive began to break through. Alan's journal writing carried some remarkable insights, not the least of which was about the intensity of the desperate spirit of competition. When he came "back to life" in Christ, it was as though he was a new person. Far wiser and healthier emotionally. Far more humble and honest. Eager to see others step into the light and to thrive. This mental and spiritual healing enabled him to become a professional life coach, and now he helps others hear the call of God.

When Pope Francis, out of genuine humility and love, chooses to wash the feet of others, to attend to the weak, to feed the poor, it isn't because he has found his call to be a pope. That was neither required nor necessary. In fact, it may have put his following Jesus under pressure. But since Francis has long followed his call to follow Jesus, now as pope he's simply continuing to do the same. The shock is that despite being pope, Francis is living as a Christian.

This should be telling for us too.

Whatever specialized and distinctly suited job or task or role God may give us, following Jesus is the first call and what should matter most. The church in Western culture is submerged in a context with endless choices that drive us to maximize self-interest at every turn. For the sincere Christian, this can easily move to an assumption that we're stymied in following God until we find that one special job or partner or activity that we think most satisfies God and us.

God gives generously and wants to use us in the wide array of settings. Sometimes, maybe often, this can include guidance in where and how we might use God's gifts to better serve the body of Christ and to live as witnesses in the world. But whether that does or doesn't happen, we already have the call that matters most: "Follow me." If we don't do that, a secondary call will not be what it was intended to be anyway. We need to get first things first.

Paul's passion was "to know Christ and the power of his resurrection and the sharing of his sufferings by becoming like him in his death, if somehow I may attain the resurrection from the dead" (Philippians 3:10-11). This is hardly the vocational vision of how to maximize the benefits of life. This is an approach to calling lived as an offering, not sought as a spiritual right. This is the call that follows in joy but also in suffering, in hope but also in doubt, in satisfaction but also in waiting.

As disciples, we can seek our particular call to serve in a specialized context, but it will really matter only if we do so in light of God's greater call to live as disciples in every context. This reveals that call is a matter of character more than of circumstances, of substance more than of form. Be a musician. Be in business. Be a manager. Be an architect. Be a parent. Be a politician. Be a friend. Be a pastor. But, above all and in all, be a disciple of Jesus.

The first thing we need to do is get clear about our primary calling as followers of Jesus, which will more than make a difference in the world. If we are clear about that, the rest of our call becomes more evident. We can give unexpected evidence of God that would not be imaginable otherwise. And that's the point. We're meant to live what is so needed and what we're distinctly meant to provide.

Not all of God's people will find the perfect job, do the work that best suits their gifts or have the chance to express their most creative and particular selves. Poverty, injustice, lack of education or opportunity, and circumstances in general keep many from such opportunity. We would want it for them and would even commit to help it become so. But for many, it's impossible.

If you're a water carrier for your family five or six hours a day, you're doing what your family most needs you to do. By circumstances and love, it is a call and it matters. If you're an undocumented worker in the United States and the only job you can get to make money for your family to survive is construction without a green card, at least it's a job, and by doing it you are serving your family and community with hard work. Through circumstances that leave you vulnerable and anxious, you can do it as an offering to God, a call to do all you can for those you love most. Maybe your particular job is one you inherited from your family and not because you chose it, but you can still do it as an offering to God and in service to others.

Or maybe you're the primary parent. It hadn't been planned this way, but your spouse's job seems more central to his or her interest than yours did to you, so you're the one at home taking care of the kids and an elderly parent. You hadn't ever pictured this as your life. You didn't feel invited into it, exactly. But you can still receive it as a gift and a doorway into loving Jesus and the neighbors God has given you.

Regardless of individual circumstances, all of God's people can live as the salt and light that they are. All of God's people can take up the calling that is our primary vocation in the world. It will be difficult to do this, of course, but difficulties are themselves the very reason the calling is so urgent and why the failure to answer the call puts so much at risk.

If we embrace and practice our primary calling to live as followers of Jesus in the most practical and ordinary contexts of our lives, the meaning of our secondary call will more likely occupy its appropriate place and will bear the weight and priority that is formed by what matters most.

If we put first things first, our sense of call will shape our character, transform how we perceive the world, and reshape how we think about and know ourselves and integrate compassion and justice in our hearts and minds. Why? Because this is what God desires and intends to do in us in order to exhibit or embody such qualities through us. This is the transformational process that enables us to live as salt and light. This is why we are called to follow.

If and when we come to a particular setting or work that especially suits the way we've been made or to work on the concerns or passions we want to give our strengths and energies to, we bring to those settings far more of what they need than just good talent or interest. We bring something of the kingdom.

God's reign opens reality in deep, creative and life-giving ways. If your first calling is primary, you bring with you the aroma of Christ's love and joy as well as the imagination and faithfulness of the God who creates and sustains. You bring resources of engagement, honesty and integrity. You bring a concern for the intrinsic value of all those you meet and a desire to do your work as an offering of yourself to God, who is redeeming all things. All this is what you bring with you from the first day.

This means that, whether we live our calling in a workplace setting or in school or in a romantic relationship or in a neighborhood or in a church or parachurch role or in some other form of advocacy and service, God's people all share the common vocation of following Jesus. We carry it out in very different ways in the challenges and opportunities of the setting we're in. Some contexts feel more natural and freeing than others. Some allow us to lose ourselves fully and easily, because we find the work more absorbing or demanding or urgent.

If our work is in the context of the church or a parachurch group, we have a great opportunity to focus our gifts in building up the body of Christ. Perhaps it seems hard for some to believe, but especially in serving the church, we need to work hard at remembering that our call is to serve the Lord of the church far more than the people of the church. Forgetting this, and forgetting that those the church serves may also forget this, is an ironic but common problem. Pastors forget all too easily that they are undershepherds to the Good Shepherd. It can be infectious, and it can make you just a bureaucrat and the church just an organization.

WHATEVER WE DO

As we live out God's call, we must continue to remember who we are, what spiritual practices keep us attentive to God and to our neighbor, and that our context is more likely exile than anywhere else. We also must remember we do this in the context of the beloved community, not alone but ever part of the wider communion of the Holy Spirit and of the fellowship we share with other believers.

Martin Luther King Jr. said, "The arc of the moral universe is long, but it bends towards justice."[2] It does so because God tends that long arc. And God wants those of us who are Jesus' disciples to live bearing witness to God's great faithfulness for a lost world.

Rather than go on as part of a lost church in that lost world, may we each and together think again about our being called to live as God's people, salt and light, in the world. As we do that, we will bear witness to the One who alone can and will make all things right, and who wants to use you and me as a part of that good work. May we live this calling day by day.

> And whatever you do, in word or deed, do everything in the name of the Lord Jesus, giving thanks to God the Father through him. (Colossians 3:17)

Practice

Form a small group of three to six people with whom you can explore the theme of personal calling. You may wish to meet together just a few times to share insights and encouragement, and to learn how to pray for one another. Or you may find this to be a helpful long-term discernment group as you walk through various seasons of your lives.

ACKNOWLEDGMENTS

This book emerges for me from decades of pastoral ministry and the privilege of walking alongside individuals and communities seeking to know and follow Jesus Christ. Much of what may be valuable in these pages has come from those people and relationships, and for all of them I am very thankful. A wide array of family, friends and strangers have helped me grow as a listener, friend and observer to wider cultural voices and attitudes, including musicians, writers, painters, filmmakers and philosophers.

It would not have been possible to write this without the help of Jennifer Ackerman. She's been instrumental from start to finish, including writing the practices and discussion questions. Her practical support, along with her suggestions and encouragement, made a world of difference.

As this book is being published, I have just completed my first year as president of Fuller Theological Seminary. I have felt God's invitation to carry this honored position in freedom and joy, and though I'm only beginning and have so much to learn, I can certainly say these words capture the experience to date. Coming to know the board of trustees, the faculty, the staff and many students inspires and challenges me to want to live and to share God's call together even more. The theme of this book is the backdrop to much of what we at Fuller are seeking to do as we help form men and women for their kingdom calling, whatever their gifts or context.

I am particularly grateful for the support of three exceptional colleagues whose input has made this book far better than it would have been otherwise: Tod Bolsinger, Scott Cormode and Doug McConnell. Many others have also been valuable conversation partners in the process, including Rob Johnston, Carmen Valdez, Aaron Graham and Kurt Labberton. Of course, I assume responsibility for the final product.

Kathryn Helmers's enthusiastic advocacy and wisdom has been so meaningful to me, and Cindy Bunch's encouragement and responsiveness has brought all the pieces together. The friendship of Bob Fryling is a gift in all these efforts.

Special thanks as always must go to my wife, Janet, whose exemplary commitment to these themes of calling is evident in so many ways, not least through her extraordinary patience and support with this project and our new life at Fuller.

NOTES

Chapter 2: A Lost Church in a Lost World

[1]"A New Generation Expresses Its Skepticism and Frustration with Christianity," www.barna.org/bama-update/teens-nextgen/94-a-new-generation-expresses-its-skepticism-and-frustration-with-christianity#.U4YMM3JdVyI, September 24, 2007.

[2]Andy Reinhardt, "Steve Jobs: There's Sanity Returning," *Business Week*, May 25, 1998, www.businessweek.com/1998/21/b3579165.htm.

Chapter 3: The Primary Call

[1]Mark Binelli, "Pope Francis: The Times They Are A-Changin,'" *Rolling Stone*, January 28, 2014, www.rollingstone.com/culture/news/pope-francis-the-times-they-are-a-changin-20140128#ixzz2tGj3fY4s.

[2]Blaise Pascal, *Blaise Pascal*, trans. W. F. Trotter (New York: P. F. Collier & Son, 1902), p. 182.

Chapter 5: Reorienting

[1]Frederick Buechner, *Wishful Thinking: A Seeker's ABC* (New York: HarperOne, 1994).

Chapter 6: Refocusing

[1]"Factoids" from *Bowling Alone*, available online at www.bowlingalone.com.

Chapter 7: The Way of the Beloved

[1]John Calvin, *Institutes of the Christian Religion* 1.1.

Chapter 10: So, What Does God Call *Me* to Do?

[1]"Exposition of Psalm 147," quoted in Gustaf Wingren, *Luther on Vocation* (Evansville, IN: Ballast Press, 1994), p. 138.

Epilogue

[1]C. S. Lewis, *The Weight of Glory: And Other Addresses* (New York: HarperCollins, 1976), p. 26.

[2]Martin Luther King Jr., a paraphrase of an original quote from abolitionist and Unitarian minister Theodore Parker (1811–1860): "Look at the facts of the world. You see a continual and progressive triumph of the right. I do not pretend to understand the moral universe; the arc is a long one, my eye reaches but little ways; I cannot calculate the curve and complete the figure by the experience of sight; I can divine it by conscience. And from what I see I am sure it bends towards justice."

Also by Mark Labberton

*The Dangerous Act
of Loving Your Neighbor*

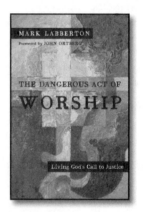

The Dangerous Act of Worship

Connect with Mark Labberton

Facebook: preslabberton

Twitter: MLabberton

Web: fuller.edu/called